£2.95

W 19

G000095306

644279 8073

# DYLAN THOMAS'S PLACES

*A biographical & literary guide*

# DYLAN THOMAS'S PLACES

## A biographical & literary guide

### JAMES A DAVIES

Christopher Davies

Copyright © James A. Davies 1987.

Published by
Christopher Davies (Publishers) Ltd.,
P.O. Box 403, Sketty,
Swansea, SA2 9BE.

*All rights reserved. No part of this publication may
be reproduced, stored in a retrieval system, or
transmitted, in any form or by any means,
electronic, mechanical, photocopying, recording
or otherwise, without the prior permission of
Christopher Davies (Publishers) Ltd.*

British Library Cataloguing in Publication Data

Davies, James A.
    Dylan Thomas's places: a biographical
    and literary guide.
    1. Thomas, Dylan — Homes and haunts
    I. Title
    821'.912        PR6039.H52Z/

    ISBN 0-7154-0654-X

*Printed in Wales by
Dynevor Printing Company,
Rawlings Road,
Llandybïe, Dyfed.*

For SOPHIE and DANIEL

# ACKNOWLEDGEMENTS

The author and publisher are grateful to J. M. Dent & Sons Ltd. and to the Trustees for the Copyrights of the late Dylan Thomas for permission to publish copyright material.

The author is grateful for help received from the following: Rowley M. Davies, Daniel Entin (Executive Director, Nicholas Roerich Museum, New York), Paul Ferris, Arthur Miller, New York Public Library (General Research Division), The Soho Society (Bryan C. Burrough), City of Swansea Archives Department, Swansea Reference Library (in particular, Lloyd Davies), City of Westminster Archives Department (Miss M. J. Swarbrick and her staff), George Evans, Mrs. G. Price, Wynn Thomas, Andrew Varney, Clive and Eileen Walton.

# CONTENTS

INTRODUCTION 1

CHRONOLOGICAL SUMMARY OF DYLAN THOMAS'S LIFE 14

PLACES
*Chapter One*
SWANSEA — 'the best place' 16

*Chapter Two*
GOWER — 'communing with . . . the quietness' 83

*Chapter Three*
LAUGHARNE — 'this wet idyllic tomb' 91

*Chapter Four*
WALES — 'the hymnal blob' 103

*Chapter Five*
LONDON — 'city of the restless dead' 131

*Chapter Six*
ENGLAND — 'This . . . flat country' 153

*Chapter Seven*
NEW YORK — 'nightmare city . . . cosy as toast' 163

*Chapter Eight*
U.S.A. — 'the gravy pots' 175

*Chapter Nine*
OTHER PLACES — Abyssinia to Zanzibar 189

PHOTOGRAPHS AND MAPS 205
EXPLANATORY NOTES 207
ABBREVIATIONS 209
FURTHER READING 210

# INTRODUCTION

Dylan Thomas is one of this century's most important literary figures. His works, those glittering products of 'craft or sullen art', are much admired and widely read. Both poetry and prose continue to attract not only the specialised literary critic but also the general reader to whom the works speak as literature of true quality has always spoken: strangely, disconcertingly, inspiringly.

Since his death in 1953 Thomas's life has become a legend even to many who have never read a word of him. It is easily summarised. As a precocious literary phenomenon he burst out of suburban and provincial Swansea during the depressed 1930s to dazzle the London literary world with the brilliant originality of his work and his ability to drink himself under every table. There, hardly prone and not always out of sight, he fornicated his way to further fame. Later he lived at Laugharne in a picturesque and slightly dilapidated boat-house with sea-views and an unruly family which he left, periodically, for roaring encounters with London and North America. In the latter, particularly in New York, the 'boily boy' plumbed new depths of infamy between wildly successful public readings given in a voice of such compelling magnificence that many still think themselves capable of poor imitations. Alcohol claimed him: he died, spectacularly, of drink, in New York City, at the romantic age of 39. Countless thousands still regard him as the typical poet and bohemian: careless of money, reputation, conventional behaviour, and the demands of polite society, obsessed only with his art, with writing, with being a poet. His behaviour retains the capacity to shock but continues to inspire envy, admiration — that is not always grudging — for Thomas's sprawling integrity, and sympathy that is certainly not lessened by the fact that his death seemed self-induced. In rejecting the world, or rather, in finally failing to reject the world, he continues to fascinate.

All legends simplify and Thomas's is no exception. One function of this book is to show the complexities of Thomas's biographical geography. Another is to show how real places are used in his writings. The guide-book format — a new approach to Thomas's life and work — enables both to be seen in new ways.

1

It must be stressed that this book is not only for the Thomas specialist. It is also for the general reader AND for the person who — as a local, tourist, visitor, or armchair traveller — is interested in places often interesting in themselves but which have acquired special significance because of their connection with a famous personality or that personality's equally-famous words.

Those places are many and varied. 'Dylan Thomas's Swansea', his 'Laugharne', his 'London', his 'New York', have predictably substantial sections. His 'Eire', his 'Italy', his 'Oxford', his imagined 'Egypt' and 'Israel', are less predictable but are demonstrably important locations. His topographical comments are often funny, sometimes outrageous, invariably striking; he has a gift for the 'quotable quote'. This book's ultimate aim is to encourage Thomas's readers to re-read and those who have never read him to start turning his pages.

*      *      *

The story of Thomas's life begins in small country places in what was, for him, Carmarthenshire and is now Dyfed. His great-uncle was a bard from Llanybydder whose bardic title, that of the nearby Marlais stream, became the boy's middle name. Thomas's father, David John ('D.J.') Thomas, was from Johnstown, his mother's family from near Llangain and Llanybri, on the road from Carmarthen to Llanstephan. As an adult Thomas recalled magical holidays in his father's birthplace, on Fernhill farm, or in the family cottages at Blaencwm, and transformed his memories into some of his greatest writings.

Schoolmastering took his father to Swansea; his mother's railwayman father also advanced from west to east, from rural to urban, in the traditional manner. Dylan's mother, Florence Williams, was born in Delhi Street, St Thomas, on Swansea's east side. When she married D. J. Thomas they set up home on the west side of the city and, shortly before Dylan Thomas was born in 1914, moved into genteel Cwmdonkin Drive, Uplands.

From this point onwards the legend has tended to take over. Yet Thomas's Swansea, the great formative influence upon him, needs careful describing. It is mainly the town-centre, the middle-class suburbs, and the western half of Swansea bay. In such areas were his comfortable home, his bookish father and indulgent mother, the chapel Sunday-schools to which he was made to go, his private school in Mirador Crescent, his Grammar School on Mount Pleasant where his father was senior English master. Young Dylan saw films at the Uplands Cinema, watched cricket at St Helen's, idled on the Sands and drank in such congenial pubs as the 'Uplands Hotel', the 'Antelope' and 'Mermaid' in Mumbles, and the 'Three Lamps' in Temple Street. Here, too, he made life-long friends with whom he whiled away his youth in cafés and pubs through beery evenings that ended with sustaining chips or breath-sweetening cashous as they swayed home to warm beds in drowsing, respectable streets.

Industrial Swansea, where huge, reeking, polluting works made the town, in the words of its Directory, 'the metallurgical centre of the world', was a foreign country rarely visited. Its odd inhabitants — tarts from Hafod, day-trippers from Brynhyfryd — were glimpsed by Thomas and his friends as occasional curiosities. Swansea's dockland was better known. As a young journalist, indeed, as an adolescent, he was attracted by a world so near in actual distance yet, in its nature, miles away from middle-class Swansea and its solidly bourgeois commercial heart. Between the wars, the Strand and the connected Docks area, parallel to High Street and Wind Street and infiltrating the old commercial areas around Gloucester Place, were alive with slums, sleazy pubs, some violence, and the sexual promise of a busy port. The journalist visited professionally; the adolescent, it is said, was attracted more by the opportunities for sinning than by those for journalistic copy. That a modern expression of civic pride — Swansea's statue of Dylan Thomas — should be sited in the Maritime Quarter, generates its own irony.

Thomas's early letters describe his reaction to what was certainly, in part, Swansea's narrow-minded provincialism, its way of thinking and behaving that seemed particularly oppressive when set against the imagined glamorous nights of metropolitan literary bohemia. Though, later, he cherished a desperate affection for his home-town, in the early 1930s he wanted only to escape.

Here the legend misleads. Thomas certainly hurtled into the literary stratosphere but, with Swansea, he made no sharp break. When, aged almost 20, he left home in 1934 to live in London, he shared a room at 5 Redcliffe Street with a Swansea friend, the painter Alfred Janes; in another room was a second boyhood friend, the painter Mervyn Levy. 'Hark, Hark

3

the Parish Pump', Thomas wrote, ruefully, to Bert Trick. In Redcliffe Street, on the outermost fringes of Chelsea, he sampled that glamorous bohemia and quickly went back home. Literary fame came quickly with *18 Poems* and *Twenty-Five Poems*, he stayed with Geoffrey Grigson in an Irish cottage, he made more visits to London, but he did not leave 5 Cwmdonkin Drive for good until he had to: in 1937 the house was sold when his parents retired to nearby Bishopston.

Marriage eventually drew him away from Swansea before the place itself changed utterly and suddenly when the town-centre was bombed flat during three February nights in 1941. Both factors fostered an already growing nostalgia for a lost world of stability and comfort.

Thomas's initial hostile attitude to Swansea is parallelled by his attitude to Wales. 'The land of my fathers. My fathers can keep it,' he wrote as he left for London in 1934. To Thomas Wales showed Swansea's provincialism on a slightly larger scale. And his knowledge of Wales was like his knowledge of Swansea: he knew very little about large parts of it. The Wales he cared for was the Wales he knew and, Swansea apart, that meant little more than Gower, Carmarthenshire, Cardiganshire and Pembroke-shire. Outside Swansea he was most at home in small rural places on or near the West Wales coast. He visited Trecynon to act with the Little Theatre but really knew as much about industrial Wales as he did about industrial Swansea. As for North Wales: here Thomas was a typical South Walian in that the North was a matter of supreme indifference to him. He made his most important visit in 1953 to write a radio talk on the International Eisteddfod at Llangollen. Though the Rev. Eli Jenkins, in *Under Milk Wood*, lists mountains and rivers from all parts of Wales in his verses in praise of Llaregyb, few were more than names to Thomas and even fewer could he probably have pronounced unaided. Wales, generally, was a mysterious place which he often visualised in terms of tourist-cliché: rugby, drinking, mining, choirs and tall-hatted women. Like his Swansea, Thomas's Wales juxtaposed the familiar with the unknown. In most of it he didn't wish much to live.

Thomas married Caitlin Macnamara in 1937 at Penzance Registry Office. Thereafter he, Caitlin, and family, pop up in surprising places. Mrs Mac-namara, his mother-in-law, lived in rural Hampshire, near Ringwood, and even bleary-eyed Thomas-seekers could have seen him strolling in the New

Forest with Caitlin and the children, or, more occasionally, drinking in Salisbury pubs. During 1944 they lived in Bosham, Sussex and Beaconsfield, Bucks: he worked for film-companies in London and, though a bowler-hatted and pin-striped Thomas was never a possibility, he did become a daily commuter to the city before deserting crowded railway platforms for an asbestos bungalow near New Quay, Dyfed. After the war the family lived in an Oxford don's summer-house and in 'Manor House' cottage in the very English Oxfordshire village of South Leigh. In 1947 they became *Signore e Signora Thomas* in a fine villa near Florence where Dylan endured the heat and the thin wine and did very little work. Then to Elba, which became a favourite place. Four years later Thomas was in Abadan as an unlikely and perspiring traveller in the Gulf to script a film — it was never completed — for Anglo-Iranian Oil.

Three places dominate these later years. The first is London. Dylan Thomas's London, like his Swansea and his Wales, has two distinct areas. It was, for Thomas, a place of business: with his bank manager in Chelsea's King's Road, his agent, David Higham, in Bedford Street, and his publisher, the gentlemanly Dent's, a few doors away. To London, as World War Two closed, Thomas commuted to earn a good salary from the film companies and regular fees from the B.B.C. In London his drinking could be stylishly located: the *Café Royal*, even its back bar, was an unlikely setting for the beery, outrageous, sometimes unwashed Swansea boy. The Savage Club, of which he was a member when he died, was an unexpected location, splendid in Carlton House Terrace; the ultra-respectable National Liberal Club was a positively bizarre refuge for the bohemian poet.

But London was also, more predictably, Paddington Station and environs, basement flats, bedsitters, and brief stays with kind and put-upon acquaintances. It meant 'Fitzrovian' pubs and the drinking-clubs of Soho. Because of the blitz it offered all-too-frequent reminders of the nearness of death. To Thomas's 'other' London of respectable business activities this had a relationship similar to that between middle-class Swansea and the Strand area: close to respectability lurked the waiting world of drunkenly-chaotic and self-indulgent living *and* dying. For Thomas, in London especially, that world did not wait long. London brought out the worst in him by enabling him to escape from fears and uncertainties into exhausting recklessness. Worst of all, in London he wrote hardly a serious line.

In the U.S.A. the same pattern was repeated, even though he went eagerly across the Atlantic seemingly to make money through respectable and orderly work. Thomas went to give public readings. John Malcolm Brinnin was his agent and made all arrangements. For the first time he had his life taken care of: hotels were provided, transport arranged, expenses paid, regular fees forthcoming. And though New York at first seemed overwhelming he came to love the Greenwich Village area, drinking regularly at the White Horse Tavern on Hudson Street, and living first near Washington Square, then, after the first visit, in rooms at the Chelsea Hotel. As Paul Ferris has shrewdly pointed out, Thomas was attracted by a part of the city that, in its proximity to the wharves of the Hudson River and more congenial scale, had some similarities to pre-war Swansea dockland.

Yet, once again, to order was juxtaposed chaos and into the latter Thomas sank through alcohol's inevitable compulsion. The boredom and loneliness of constant travelling, the lionising, the profuse provision of spirits as distinct from beer, let alone his fears of losing his gifts, of public performances, of strange places and demanding people, all fuelled an impulse towards destruction that had long — perhaps always — lurked in the poet's subconscious mind. The U.S.A. provided his best opportunity for such suicidal sinking and there, inevitably, he drank himself to death.

Laugharne, the third and final dominant place, was different. For most it means the Boat House and the brooding poet forever frozen on a sea-backed balcony or turning quizzically to camera in his Work-Hut study. In reality, his links with Laugharne are more complicated. He first visited in 1934 and first stayed there, with Caitlin, at the Georgian house next to the Castle belonging to Richard Hughes, the successful author of *A High Wind in Jamaica*. The Thomases lived in a damp yet waterless house called *'Eros'*, in Gosport Street, then in the larger *'Sea View'* near the Castle. Only in 1949 did they return to Laugharne to live, for the rest of Thomas's life, at his most famous address.

In Laugharne he found a kind of happiness. In his Boat House years he brought his aged parents to live in King Street, opposite Brown's Hotel, and visited them daily. Indeed, this isolated community — at once eccentric, tolerant, kindly — was most valuable for Thomas in imposing upon him a congenial routine. He pottered in the mornings before calling on his parents, drank through long lunchtimes in Brown's Hotel, ate late, then worked through the slow afternoons in his shack until, in the middle evening, the pub called again and he answered if not with alacrity at least with an unfailing determination. Laugharne was supportive, spiritually and practically — the infant Colm was left with a local woman when Caitlin accompanied Thomas to America in 1952 — and through drizzly, sleepy days he wrote some good poems and began *Under Milk Wood*, his play about the place.

Unlike Swansea, London, and the U.S.A., Laugharne was not, for Thomas, a place of two parts. But it remained only one part of his whole life and, as such, juxtaposed to the beckoning chaos now mainly across the Atlantic, could not satisfy his every need and, so, could not contain him. He left Laugharne too eagerly and once too often.

*      *      *

Literature, of course, is not life but a version of it, a response to it. Nowhere is this more apparent than in literature's treatment of 'place'. This last is always subjective: Dickens and Thackeray both wrote of mid-Victorian London and sometimes walked together through it, yet, for Dickens, it was a city of labyrinthine streets, fog and threatening darkness, and, for Thackeray, a series of elegant façades. Thus a distinction is necessary between the real places of Thomas's life and the 'real' places mentioned or described in his creative work. The 'Swansea' of the *Portrait* stories, the 'London' of the war poems or of *Adventures in the Skin Trade*, the 'Laugharne' of *Under Milk Wood*, are those towns and cities essentially transformed by the author's imagination.

In his early stories Thomas works outside the restrictions of recognisable locations. He invents places, only vaguely and fantastically Welsh, such as Aberbabel and LlanAsia and, most notoriously, Llareggub. More importantly, in stories published during the 1930s and collected in *The Map of Love* (1939) — such stories as 'The Holy Six', 'The Tree', 'The Enemies', 'The Map of Love' — Thomas creates strange, rural worlds in a mysterious, unlocated Welsh countryside.

One such world is called 'Cader', perhaps loosely linked to the Cader Idris area of North Wales. 'Cader' has a chapel, house, marshes, peak and lake, but the topography is never clearly visualised. What Thomas wanted was a setting sufficiently unfamiliar to contain the mixture of black magic and nightmarish sex and violence that fills his earlier fiction, and North Wales would do. 'Cader' is one response to rural Wales — 'out there' and 'up North' anything can happen — 'Jarvis' is another. Thomas tried, as he told Pamela Hansford Johnson, to write a novel about 'the Jarvis valley', but though that came to nothing the valley itself, the 'Jarvis hills', and the 'Jarvis wilderness', are the imaginary settings of parts of 'The Holy Six', 'The Enemies' and 'The Visitor'. The people of 'Jarvis', it has to be said, behave as oddly as the inhabitants of 'Cader'.

As for Thomas's early poetry: in the famous *Notebooks* filled, mainly, in the back bedroom of 5 Cwmdonkin Drive and containing first drafts of so many famous poems, 'Cader' and 'Jarvis' find their poetic equivalents in a series of exotic references and settings. For example, 'Hassan's Journey into the World' is set in an Arabia awash — the metaphor is chosen with care — with beautiful and adventurous women. And Thomas is fascinated by ancient Egypt's paradoxical mixture of Nile-based fertility and an obsession with death: 'Osiris, Come to Isis' is another adolescent version of young love in a moist place. Egypt appears again in 'Should Lanterns Shine', a far finer work two lines of which point to his conception of Egypt as a place of funereal sexuality:

> And from her lips the faded pigments fall,
> And mummy cloths expose an ancient breast.

A turning-point in Thomas's work came in the late 1930s when Richard Church of Dent's suggested the abandonment of the strange, neo-surrealistic, vibrantly-sexual, unlocated stories for more realistic material. The result was, as Thomas told Vernon Watkins, 'a series of short, straightforward stories about Swansea' that became *Portrait of the Artist as a Young Dog* (1940). In his poetry Thomas had already turned away from middle-eastern and other fantasies so that, from this point onwards, his work reflects a sense of place and most of his best work — the *Portrait* stories, 'The Hunchback in the Park', 'Fern Hill', are three examples — is precisely located.

Much of the rest of this introduction is about 'Swansea', 'London', and 'Laugharne', as they appear in Thomas's creative writings. These places, above all, exercised a profound effect upon his imagination. In relation to 'Swansea' that imagination seized upon one aspect of his own experience —

the juxtaposition of the respectable with the sordid, High Street with the Strand — and turned it into an artistic principle clearly seen in two of his finest stories.

'One Warm Saturday', written in 1938 and the conclusion of *Portrait of the Artist as a Young Dog*, is a superb study of adolescent loneliness. The narrator, a 'young man' sometimes called 'Jack', is alone on Swansea's crowded sands on a summer Saturday. His friends are elsewhere; he has chosen to spend a solitary day. In the early evening he sees a girl in nearby Victoria Gardens (see Victoria Park) and again, with friends, in the nearby 'Victoria saloon' (based on the Bay View Hotel). The young man becomes part of her group, which includes an Irishman with a motor-car. The girl, named 'Lou', makes advances to the young man. At closing-time the Irishman drives them all to Lou's room in a tenement-block on the other side of the town. The group pairs off, the young man, eagerly, with Lou. But the evening's drinking forces him to search for a lavatory. He loses his way in the building and never finds his desperate way back to Lou's room. The story ends with him stumbling hopelessly away across an adjoining demolition-site.

'Old Garbo', also a *Portrait* story, begins in the offices of a Swansea newspaper. The first part describes young Thomas at work as a journalist and having coffee with his friends in a High Street cafe. But the story is mainly about a pub-crawl with Mr Farr, the hard-bitten senior reporter, that begins among respectable professional men in the 'Three Lamps' in Temple Street, at the heart of pre-war Swansea's business district, and continues in sleazy pubs in the Strand and elsewhere. Young Thomas becomes drunk and remains fascinated by the low life he has suddenly glimpsed. The story ends days later with him making a further visit, alone, to the 'Fishguard Arms' in the Strand and with his continuing confusion about the happenings of his night out with Mr Farr.

A key sequence, for both stories, occurs in the second. In the 'Three Lamps' Mr Farr and young Thomas are 'safe in a prosperous house', drinking 'lazily in the company of business and professional men'; after only a short walk and a brief call at the 'Carlton Hotel', they 'crawled down Strand alleys by the side of the mortuary, through a gas-lit lane where hidden babies cried together', to reach the 'Fishguard Arms'. Thomas's main concern is with the narrowness of the dividing-line between two such different worlds. Both stories begin in the familiar, precisely-located, and reassuring surroundings of middle-class Swansea, and with controlled patterns of behaviour; both stories show the young hero sliding swiftly into the unlocated and the confusing, into darkness, chaos and failure.

Three famous 'Swansea' poems have the same basic structure. 'Why east wind chills', which Thomas wrote after hearing a question asked by the daughter of his friend, Bert Trick, and which has memories of the Grammar School in its closing lines, charts a movement from an adult's acceptance of the limitations of knowledge — a limited but controlled position — to a sense of inadequacy and the beginnings of confusion. A second poem, 'Once it was the colour of saying', describes the transition from the reassuring certainties of Thomas's early career as a poet to a hard and disturbing present. 'The hunchback in the park', one of the best-known of Thomas's poems, contrasts the man in Cwmdonkin Park, sustained by his imagination even though tormented by boys, with the dreadful and unlocated 'kennel in the dark' for which, each evening, he has to leave. 'Return Journey', that marvellous evocation of lost, pre-blitz Swansea and Thomas when young, enacts the same disturbing shift: the familiar landmarks, the ordered behaviour of a Swansea upbringing, are overwhelmed, inevitably, by the unplaced darkness of death.

London is treated differently in Thomas's creative work. *Adventures in the Skin Trade* begins in respectable Swansea, in Cwmdonkin Drive disguised as Mortimer Street, but its 'London' is simply chaos and failure. The novel is unfinished and this is hardly surprising. Its movement towards nightmare is too powerful to impose artistic order. The last completed section, the aptly named 'Four Lost Souls', ends with a description of Londoners as beasts and grotesques which combines hatred, fascination and fear. Little wonder the novel could not be continued.

A further response to London is made in the five war poems: 'Deaths and Entrances', 'Among those Killed in the Dawn Raid was a Man Aged a Hundred', 'Ceremony After a Fire Raid', 'A Refusal to Mourn the Death, by Fire, of a Child in London', and 'Holy Spring'. These attempts to come to terms with the cruel chaos of war and of bombed London seek to celebrate the survival of the human and religious values of the city and its inhabitants through the darkest days of death and destruction. But a sense of strain is only too apparent: even the celebratory final section of 'Ceremony After a Fire Raid' has its optimism at least partly undermined by a final line in which the use of the word 'sundering' leaves the reader with a disturbing reminder of death. Thomas's most persuasive portrayal of 'London' remains the nightmare vision of *Adventures in the Skin Trade*.

In Thomas's 'London' happiness is a rare commodity; in his 'Laugharne' it is a staple ingredient. In such poems as 'When I woke', 'Over Sir John's Hill', 'Poem on his Birthday', and 'Prologue', the small Carmarthenshire town in its beautiful landscape is transformed into a profoundly harmonious world. Death is present, of course, but is accepted as part of the natural process, even, perhaps, desired as a peaceful end to living. 'As I sail out to die', the final line of 'Poem on his Birthday', that celebration of the poet in his 'Laugharne' setting, is, in its heroic eagerness, a very different kind of line from, say, 'To his kennel in the dark', in that sad poem on the hunchback's unavoidable fate. The close of *Under Milk Wood* — the 'Laugharne' work above all others — with its beautiful, consoling, awakening darkness, is a world away from the hopelessness of the conclusion to 'One Warm Saturday'. In Thomas's work 'Laugharne' is a potent place, the luminous setting for a graceful progress through life to death.

*          *          *

In his sense of place and in his use of places Dylan Thomas is part of a great literary tradition to which, for example, Dickens's London, Hardy's Wessex, and Joyce's Dublin also belong. Like them he is usually accurate in his topographical references.

Only occasionally is such accuracy subverted: 'Marlborough', for instance, is a fictitious name that almost certainly disguises a real pub in central pre-war Swansea. In 'The Peaches', the story that opens *Portrait of the Artist as a Young Dog*, Uncle Jim leaves his cart between two pubs in Swansea's Union Street, 'The Pure Drop' and 'The Hare's Foot'. Both may mask real places but, almost certainly, Thomas is more interested, here, in the satirical force of the names: the former speaks for itself in a pre-war Wales of lingering temperance movements, and the latter is an obvious comic development of 'the hair of the dog'. Sometimes the Welsh language is used to make humorous points, as with Cathmarw and Twll; the mindless intoning of so many obscure Welsh rivers and mountains by the Reverend Eli Jenkins in *Under Milk Wood* may also be Thomas's idea of a joke. In 'Old

11

Garbo', the *Portrait* story, the townscape itself seems, on occasion, to be a further source of private — or, at least, local — humour: from Swansea's High Street the young reporter takes a 'short cut' back to the newspaper office in Castle Street by going in the opposite direction up High Street, down Chapel Street and back down the Strand.

These are minor aberrations. The only major deviation from coherent topography occurs in 'The Followers'. This short story begins in a central Swansea street given the fictitious name of Crimea Street, moves to the 'Marlborough' and then through Crimea Street to what is almost certainly the Uplands Cinema. The two young men follow a girl through Inkerman Street — in reality, across the river in east-side St Thomas — and Paradise Passage (certainly a false name for Salubrious Passage off Wind Street) only to find themselves in what seems to be St Helen's Crescent — here disguised as St Augustus Crescent — and an avenue that can only be St Helen's Avenue, before separating at Victoria Corner.

An author is under no obligation to be factually accurate. But Thomas usually is; in 'The Followers' readers are encouraged to think that he will be, because he does use *some* real place-names. The blurred topography may, of course, be another joke, but it is worth remembering that this is a very late story: it was published and probably written in 1952, many years after the *Portrait* stories which it resembles. Significantly, it is about looking-in, about not properly belonging, and this theme seems emphasised by Thomas's inability to recreate accurately a pre-war Swansea faded by time and partly destroyed by German bombs. The theme is no less emphatic if what we have here is simply a loss of interest in topographical clarity. Certainly, in this story — in the last eighteen months of Thomas's life — his home town ceases to be a coherent entity, a reassuringly familiar presence. The imagined 'Laugharne' had become his final vulnerable fortress.

*       *       *

Thomas's world has changed; parts have gone. Central Swansea was blitzed, areas of London blitzed or redeveloped, New York constantly changed. But, as Tennyson said, 'Though much is taken, much abides', and though he wasn't referring to buildings the sentiment is worth remembering. Rather than being appalled by what has been lost we can be pleasantly surprised by the amount that still survives. Cwmdonkin was not blitzed, neither were Uplands, Sketty, Mumbles and Gower. Swansea's bay also remains; the sea is still the sea. In London the Welsh visitor still arrives at a Paddington Station basically unchanged since Thomas's first glimpse of the bar in the buffet; 54 Delancey Street, Camden Town, now has a blue plaque commemorating the Thomas family's short stay there and is still a house they would have recognised; many of his London pubs have proved to be indestructible. In New York the Chelsea Hotel also has a plaque and survives in the old style; the White Horse Tavern has a picture of Thomas in the bar-room and one suspects that in any reincarnation he would still drink their drinks; Greenwich Village still has an atmosphere to which he would have responded. The Boat House at Laugharne is now a museum but looks much as it did; Laugharne itself will always be a 'timeless, mild, beguiling island of a town' set in a sleepy landscape.

And Dylan Thomas's places still reveal themselves in odd moments, in sudden glimpses. The drizzling rain sweeping into Cwmdonkin Park from a Swansea Bay where foghorns still drone, pre-war remains above modern shop-fronts in Swansea's High Street and Wind Street, the sounds of drinkers in those famous Mumbles pubs, the sweep of Rhossilli, Worm's Head in a sparkling sea, the 'Fitzroy' in London's Charlotte Street on a rainy winter's evening, spring in New York with a cold wind blowing off the Hudson, Laugharne full of sunshine and asleep despite the tourists — such sights, such moments 'in and out of time', bring back that 'bulging apple' of a man and enhance the living landscapes of his works.

# CHRONOLOGICAL SUMMARY OF DYLAN THOMAS'S LIFE

| | |
|---|---|
| 1876 | Father born at Johnstown, Dyfed. |
| 1882 | Mother born at 29 Delhi Street, St Thomas, Swansea. |
| 1914 | Dylan Thomas born at 5 Cwmdonkin Drive, Uplands, Swansea. |
| 1925-31 | Attended Swansea Grammar School, where his father was senior English master. |
| 1931-32 | Junior reporter on *South Wales Daily* (later *Evening*) *Post*. |
| 1933 | Began corresponding with Pamela Hansford Johnson. |
| | His first poems published in London. |
| | His first visit to London. |
| 1934 | Stayed with the Johnsons at 53 Battersea Rise, S.W.11. |
| | First lived in London, at 5 Redcliffe Street, S.W.10. |
| | *18 Poems* (*Sunday Referee*/Parton Press). |
| 1936 | Met Caitlin Macnamara in 'The Wheatsheaf', Rathbone Place, W.1. |
| | *Twenty Five Poems* (Dent). |
| 1937 | Married Caitlin Macnamara at Penzance Registry Office. |
| 1938 | First lived in Laugharne. |
| 1939 | Elder son, Llewellyn, born at Poole, Dorset. |
| | *The Map of Love* (Dent). |
| | First published in the U.S.A.: *The World I Breathe* (Norfolk, Conn.: New Directions). |
| 1940 | *Portrait of the Artist as a Young Dog* (Dent). |
| | Moved back to London. |
| | Began script-writing for film companies. |
| 1940-41 | *The Death of the King's Canary* (with John Davenport)— not published in full until 1976. |
| 1943 | Daughter, Aeronwy, born in London. |
| | Broadcasting for the B.B.C. |
| | *New Poems* (Norfolk, Conn.: New Directions). |
| 1944-45 | Lived in New Quay, Dyfed. |
| 1946 | *Deaths and Entrances* (Dent). |
| | *Selected Writings of Dylan Thomas* (New York: New Directions). |

| | |
|---|---|
| 1946–49 | Lived in Oxford and in South Leigh, Oxfordshire. |
| 1947 | Lived in Italy. |
| 1949 | Visited Prague. |
| | Began living at The Boat House, Laugharne. |
| | Second son, Colm, born in Carmarthen. |
| 1950 | First American visit. |
| 1952 | Second American visit, with Caitlin. |
| | *In Country Sleep* (New York: New Directions) |
| | *Collected Poems* (Dent). |
| | Death of his father. |
| 1953 | Third American visit. |
| | First performance, in New York, of *Under Milk Wood*. |
| 1953 | Began final American visit. |
| (Oct. — | Died in New York City. |
| (Nov.) | Buried in Laugharne. |

CHAPTER ONE

# SWANSEA

# 'the best place'

*Swansea Town Centre (Pre-War)*

18

As the INTRODUCTION indicates, Swansea was Thomas's home town (it became a city only in 1969) where he was born, bred, educated, worked briefly as a journalist, and wrote much poetry. In the 1920s and 1930s it was a drab town in a beautiful setting, the irregular and spectacular crescent of Swansea Bay. Until November 1934 he hardly left it but grew increasingly ill-at-ease with what he considered to be its chapel-dominated provincialism. He was always a writer; his birthplace made him a rebellious one. The brilliant originality of his work can be seen, at least in part, as a consequence of that early desire to be different.

Thomas never wholly broke away from Swansea: he kept returning and referring to it. And as, away from Swansea, his life began to dissolve into chaos he came, more and more, to value his roots. His letters show that as early as 1938 he had begun to idealize Swansea with a desperate affection. Nine years later, and six years after the German bombing raids of 1941, he put his feelings for Swansea into 'Return Journey', that marvellous, moving evocation of his lost youth in a lost town.

The following poems, stories, and other writings, make use, either wholly or in part, of recognizable Swansea settings (occasionally the town is called 'Tawe', 'Abertawe' ('the mouth of the river Tawe') being, of course, its Welsh name:

(a) *Poems*
    'Rain cuts the place we tread'
    'The spire cranes' (possibly: see *St Thomas's Church*, below)
    'Upon your held-out hand'
    'I have longed to move away'
    'Poet: 1935'
    'Why east wind chills'
    'Greek Play in a Garden'
    'Ears in the turrets hear'
    'Especially when the October wind'
    'Should lanterns shine'
    'Once it was the colour of saying'
    'The hunchback in the park'

(b) *Fiction*

*Portrait of the Artist as a Young Dog* (except for 'A Visit to Grandpa's' and 'Extraordinary Little Cough')

*Adventures in the Skin Trade* (the first two parts of 'A Fine Beginning')

'A Child's Christmas in Wales' (incorporating 'Conversations about Christmas' and 'Memories of Christmas')

'Holiday Memory'

'Return Journey'

'The Followers'

(c) *Other Writings*

'The Poets of Swansea'

'Reminiscences of Childhood'

# REFERENCES TO SWANSEA

## Letters

(i) For Trevor Hughes, see *Gorse Terrace*, below, and Chapter Five / *Rayner's Lane, Harrow*. During 1932 he had left Swansea to live and work in Harrow. Thomas's letters discuss literary matters — Hughes also wished to be a writer — and, usually, disparage his home town: 'Swansea still stands where it did. No one has blown up the churches.'
[*CL*, 14: to Trevor Hughes (February 1933)].

(ii) Grigson had recently founded *New Verse* which, under his editorship, became one of the most distinguished literary magazines of its day. Thomas's first poems were returned; he sent them with a note on the problems of living in 'the smug darkness of a provincial town'.
[*CL*, 19: to Geoffrey Grigson (Summer 1933)].

(iii) For Pamela Hansford Johnson, see Chapter Five / *53 Battersea Rise, S.W.11*. Thomas corresponded with her for some months before they met in London during February 1934. His letters include lengthy descriptions of 'this blowsy town . . . a dingy hell'.
[*CL*, 62-3: to Pamela Hansford Johnson (early December 1933)].

(iv) Under A. E. Trick's influence (see *69 Glanbrydan Avenue*, below) Thomas's letter to the editor is mainly concerned to attack fascism. It opens in more familiar territory:
'In this overpeopled breeding box of ours, this ugly contradiction of a town for ever compromised between the stacks and the littered bays, the Philistines exercise an inevitable dictatorship'.
[*CL*, 142: to the Editor, *Swansea and West Wales Guardian* (8 June 1934)].

(v) Now 'unofficially engaged', Thomas urges his 'fiancée' to visit Swansea. She came, with her mother, in September 1934, for an unsuccessful visit that began the end of the affair. Certainly he cannot be accused of exaggerating his town's attractions, with its 'shabby, badly built streets. Unutterable melancholy blowing along the tramlines'.
[*CL*. 145: to Pamela Hanford Johnson (early July 1934)].

(vi) During 1935 Thomas alternated between Swansea and London. To the Merthyr-born and Cardiff-based teacher and writer who had become a friend he describes Swansea as a comfortable but lonelier place.
[*CL*, 186: to Glyn Jones (early March 1935)].

(vii) Heppenstall, poet and novelist, was one of Thomas's London drinking companions. Thomas, back in Swansea for Christmas, now lives 'a comfortable, sheltered, and, now, only occasionally boozy life'.

21

[*CL*, 208: to Rayner Heppenstall (31 December 1935)].

(viii) From Ringwood, Hampshire, where Dylan and Caitlin were staying with her mother, he writes wistfully to an old and close Swansea friend and former fellow-journalist:
'Swansea is still the best place . . . I'll set up . . . in a neat villa full of drinks and pianos and lawnmowers and dumb-bells'.
[*CL*, 271: to Charles Fisher (11 February 1938)].

(ix) Again from Ringwood, Thomas writes of Swansea as a place where he now feels less happy and comfortable.
[*CL*, 363-5: to Bert Trick (March 1939)].

(x) From Seaview, Laugharne (see Chapter Three), Thomas looks forward to a Christmas visit to 'our beautiful drab town . . . I want to hear the sweet town accent float into my ears like the noise of old brakes'.
[*CL*, 434: to Charles Fisher (December 1939)].

(xi) With his Christmas visit in mind Thomas describes Swansea, ecstatically, as his 'marble-town, city of laughter, little Dublin'.
[*CL*, 435: (13 December 1939)].

## *Works*

(i) The young man feels ordinary, shabby, vital Tawe life pressing upon him.
['One Warm Saturday', *Portrait*, *CS*, 225].

(ii) The young man's adventures have been among 'the small and hardly known and never-to-be-forgotten people of the dirty town'.
['One Warm Saturday', *Portrait*, *CS*, 238].

(iii) (a) The young Dylan, waiting for his uncle Jim to leave the pub, thinks of his warm bed with 'sleepy midnight Swansea flowing and rolling round outside the house'.
(b) Jack Williams, Dylan's best friend, arrives from Swansea to stay at 'Gorsehill' farm.
['The Peaches', *Portrait*, *CS*, 123, 129].

(iv) Thomas, the young journalist, includes 'Tawe' in his extended address.
['Old Garbo', *Portrait*, *CS*, 210].

(v) *Where Tawe Flows* is the novel on which young Mr Thomas and his friends are collaborating. The novel's heroine, Mary Phillips, shows the hero her parents' collection of Swansea china.
['Where Tawe Flows', *Portrait*, *CS*, 189].

(vi) Mr Jenkyn and Mr Morris discuss a performance of *The Messiah* given by Swansea and District Male Voice Choir.
['The Fight', *Portrait*, CS, 161].
(vii) A 'sprawling, submerged town', thinks the escaping Samuel Bennet.
['A Fine Beginning', *ST*, *CS*, 240].
(viii) 'an ugly, lovely town . . . crawling, sprawling, slummed, unplanned, jerry-villa'd, and smug-suburbed by the side of a long and splendidly-curving shore'.
['Reminiscences of Childhood (First Version)', *QEOM*, 1].
(ix) 'the stained and royal town . . . the still homes over the mumbling bay'.
['Holiday Memory', *CS*, 304, 310].
(x) 'the dizzy, ditchwater town at the end of the railway lines'.
['The Followers', *CS*, 331].
(xi) 'Billy Swansea with the dog's voice' is one of the playing children heard by Captain Cat.
[*UMW*, 38].

## 60 Alexandra Road

Ralph Wishart's bookshop. 'Ralph-the-books' was a staunch friend of Thomas's. This shop became a newsagent's, the bookshop having moved to Dillwyn Street a few years before Ralph Wishart's death.

Map 1 (p. 18) & Map 3 (p. 77).

## Antelope Hotel, Mumbles Road, Mumbles

A favourite haunt of Thomas's, being, then, conveniently near the Little Theatre.

Map 6 (p. 80).

## Arches, Oystermouth Road & Mumbles Road

These were entrances to the beach under the L.M.S. railway line that once skirted part of Swansea Bay.

See *Brynmill Arch* and *Trafalgar Arch*, below.

The Promenade-Man recalls young Thomas dawdling in them.

['Return Journey', *CS*, 325].

*Antelope Hotel*

*Ben Evans & Co. Ltd.*

*Bay View Hotel*

## Bay View Hotel, Oystermouth Road

(i)  The young narrator, loitering in cold
     Trafalgar Arch, wishes he was there:
     'the public bar of the "Bay View" at
     the corner had a fire and skittles and a
     swarthy, sensuous girl with different
     coloured eyes'.
     ['Just Like Little Dogs', *Portrait, CS*,
     175].
(ii) Thinly disguised as the ' "Victoria"
     saloon', the 'Bay View' is the setting
     of part of the story.
     ['One Warm Saturday', *Portrait, CS*,
     222-31].

Map 4 (p. 78).

## Ben Evans & Co. Ltd., Castle Bailey Street

Swansea's biggest and best department-
store until destroyed in the 1941 blitz.

(i)  Gwyneth, one of the girl campers, is,
     thinks the narrator, 'as immaculate
     and unapproachable as a girl in Ben
     Evans' stores'.
     ['Extraordinary Little Cough', *Por-
     trait, CS*, 170-1].
(ii) The man in the pub asks the narrator
     if he remembers the destroyed shop.
     ['Return Journey', *CS*, 319].

Map 1 (p. 18).

## Bethesda Welsh Baptist Chapel, Prince of Wales Road

(i)   Mrs Dacey seems such a pillar of the
      church that her head could support
      Bethesda.
      ['Four Lost Souls', *ST, CS*, 281].
(ii)  'Eunuchs struck gongs the size of
      Bethesda Chapel'.
      ['Quite Early One Morning', *CS*,
      292].
(iii) Young Thomas is terrified by a story
      of boys lost in the snow near
      Bethesda.
      ['Memories of Christmas', *QEOM*,
      27].
(iv)  Where Thomas, the young journalist,
      reports a bazaar.
      ['Return Journey', *CS*, 321].
(v)   This late reference is to an imaginary
      chapel in an unlocated story.
      ['A Story', *CS, 338*].

Map 3 (p. 77).

## Black Boy Inn, 444 Gower Road, Killay

The name of this pub is given to the
imaginary pub in London's Shepherd's
Bush that is used by Ted Jackson.
['The Londoner', *The Doctor and the Devils
and Other Scripts*, 216, 227-8].

Map 5 (p. 79).

*Bethesda Chapel in 1986*

**Bristol Channel**
'There is a foghorn crying out to the ships in the Bristol Channel as an albatross might have cried to the ancient mariner'. [CL, 82: to Pamela Hansford Johnson (25 December 1933)].

**British Legion, 73 Mansel Street**
Where Thomas, the young reporter, calls. ['Return Journey', CS, 321]. Map 3 (p. 77).

**Brynhyfryd**
A residential and industrial suburb north of the city centre.
On the pleasure-boat to Ilfracombe,

Ronald is 'in the thick saloon, with a party from Brynhyfryd'. ['One Warm Saturday', *Portrait*, CS, 221].

**Brynmill**
A residential area between Uplands and the beach.
Where Arnold thought Edith worked. ['Patricia, Edith, and Arnold, *Portrait*, CS, 149]. Map 4 (p. 78).

**Brynmill Arch**
The railway arch — now simply the entrance to the beach — opposite the junction of Brynmill Lane and Mumbles Road.

*Brynmill Arch in 1936*

Where the Narrator sometimes stood.
['Just Like Little Dogs', *Portrait*, *CS*, 176].
Map 4 (p. 78).

*Brynmill Terrace (now Lower Brynmill Lane)*
The Narrator moves from the sea through Brynmill Terrace on his way to the Uplands.
['Return Journey', *CS*, 326].
Map 4 (p. 78).

*Bugle, High Street*
An unidentified pub.
Mr Evans is seen entering through the side-door.
['Old Garbo', *Portrait*, *CS*, 209].

*Bush Hotel, High Street*
Thomas sometimes stayed here when visiting Swansea and occasionally drank here.
Map 1 (p. 18) & Map 3 (p. 77).

*Café Royal, High Street*
Thomas's description of the 'Café Royal' is probably of the 'Kardomah'. *Possibly* the Café Royal was part of the Royal Hotel, High Street, all of which was destroyed by bombs.

Thomas, the young reporter, describes the cafe as a favourite meeting-place for young office and shop workers.
['Old Garbo', *Portrait*, *CS*, 207].
Map 1 (p. 18).

*Swansea Castle*

### Carlton Hotel, Oxford Street
This has not been positively identified; it may well have been part of the Carlton Cinema / Empire Theatre complex.

(a) Its barmaid's attractions are stressed by Thomas's friend Leslie Bird.

(b) Near the 'Carlton' was a public convenience outside which young Thomas is winked at by a girl.

(c) After drinking rum he feels he could 'roll the "Carlton" barmaid, like a barrel' along the sands.
['Old Garbo', *Portrait, CS*, 209, 212, 214].
Map 3 (p. 77).

### Castle
'the fragment of the Castle'.

['Return Journey', *CS*, 321].
Map 1 (p. 18) & Map 3 (p. 77).

### Castle Street
The Narrator of 'Return Journey' walks down bombed Castle Street and remembers a few of the bombed shops and offices in Castle Street, Castle Square and Temple Street: Price's Fifty Shilling, Crouch the Jeweller, Potter Gilmore Gowns, Evans Jeweller, Master's Outfitters, Style and Mantle, Lennard's Boots, True Form, Kardomah, R. E. Jones, Dean's Tailor, David Evans, Gregory Confectioners, Bovega, Burton's, Lloyds Bank.
['Return Journey', *CS*, 319].
Map 1 (p. 18) & Map 3 (p. 77).

*Castle Street with 'Kardomah'*

*Castle Street Congregational Church*
Destroyed. Thomas's parents were married here on 30 December 1903.
Map 1 (p. 18).

*Cefn Coed Psychiatric Hospital, Tycoch*
*Letters:*
(i)  '. . . like a snail with the two turrets of its water towers two snails' horns'.
     [*CL*, 18-19: to Trevor Hughes (Summer 1933)].
(ii) Included in Thomas's list of Swansea's main features.
     [*CL*, 146: to Pamela Hansford Johnson (early July 1934)].
*Work:*
(i)  'The new asylum on the hill
     Leers down the valley like a fool'.

['Upon your held-out hand', *PDJ*, 33; *Notebooks*, 158].
Map 5 (p. 79).

*Cenotaph, Esplanade, Mumbles Road*
Where the Narrator meets Promenade-Man.
['Return Journey', *CS*, 325].
Map 2 (p. 76).

*Chapel Street*
(i)  For young Thomas it is an improbably short cut from High Street to the newspaper office.
     ['Old Garbo', *Portrait*, *CS*, 209].
(ii) Where Samuel Bennet's mother had her photograph taken.
     ['A Fine Beginning', *ST*, *CS*, 240].
Map 1 (p. 18).

*Cenotaph and Esplanade*

### Clevedon College, Cwmdonkin Drive
Once a private school for girls the build-
ing has now been demolished and the site
redeveloped as housing.
See also, *Cwmdonkin Drive*, below.
Where girls played on a sloping field.
['Once it was the colour of saying', *PDJ*,
144].
Map 4 (p. 78).

### College Street
The Narrator walks through bombed
College Street and lists some of the
destroyed buildings in College Street and
Castle Street: Langley's, Castle Cigar
Co., T. B. Brown, Pullar's, Aubrey Jere-
miah, Goddard Jones, Richards, Hornes,
Marles, Pleasaunce & Harper, Star
Supply, Sidney Heath, Wesley Chapel.
['Return Journey', *CS*, 323].
Map 1 (p. 18).

### Compass/Compasses Hotel
This has not been positively identified; it
may be a reference to the Compass
Tavern (which became the 'Nag's Head')
in Goat Street.
(i)  Mrs Parsons was seen 'coming out of
     the Compass piggyback on a drunk
     sailor, catching pennies in her
     garters'.
     ['A Fine Beginning', *ST*, *CS*, 241].
(ii) Women in a London Club remind
     Samuel Bennet of those in the Com-
     passes' off-licence.
     ['Four Lost Souls', *ST*, *CS*, 285].

(iii) Where Leslie and the narrator decide not to go.
['The Followers', *CS*, 330].
Map 1 (p. 18).


*Convent School, St James's Crescent*
Then St Winifride's R.C. School, now a private school called Ffynone House.
Young Dylan, waiting in the cold for his uncle to leave the pub, thinks wistfully of 'a tall, wise, golden royal girl from Swansea convent'.
['The Peaches', *Portrait*, *CS*, 123].
Map 4 (p. 78).


*Crimea Street*
Unidentified; there has been no Swansea street with this name.
The narrator meets Leslie on the corner.
['The Followers', *CS*, 330].


*Cwmbwrla*
A working-class area north of the city centre.
See Chapter Five/*Soho*.


*Cwmdonkin*
A middle-class, residential area of Swansea — part of the Uplands — in which Thomas was born and bred.
*Letters:*
(i) Thomas describes 'Once it was the colour of saying' as his 'Cwmdonkin Poem'.
[*CL*, 347 (29 December 1938)].
(ii) In a letter from Hampshire 'Cwmdonkin sonnets' are recalled.
[*CL*, 364: to Bert Trick (March 1939)].

*Works:*
(i) The setting of the story.
['Patricia, Edith, and Arnold', *Portrait*, *CS*, 144-52].
(ii) Described satirically as a place of mown lawns and badly-built 'trim villas'.
['The Countryman's Return', *PDJ*, 156].
Map 4 (p. 78).


*Cwmdonkin Drive*
A very steep street overlooking Swansea Bay and the Bristol Channel. In Thomas's day there were houses on only one side; on the other was *Clevedon College* (see above) with tall trees and, sometimes, grazing sheep in its grounds. Behind the College was Cwmdonkin Park.
*Letters:*
(i) 'this respectable Drive'.
[*CL*, 113: to Pamela Hansford Johnson (15 April 1934)].
(ii) 'coughing sheep . . . plague my life'.
[*CL*, 109: to Pamela Hansford Johnson (late March 1934)].
(iii) 'a treed hill, field on one side, houses on the other'.
[*CL*, 146: to Pamela Hansford Johnson (early July 1934)].
(iv) He describes himself as 'belly-churning Thomas, the Rimbaud of Cwmdonkin Drive'.
[*CL*, 487 (28 May 1941)].
*Works:*
(i) The poet recalls the trees and the sheep.
['Upon your held-out hand', *PDJ*, 33; *Notebooks*, 158].
(ii) 'the uglier side of a hill
With a capsized field where a
school sat still'.

*Cwmdonkin Drive in 1986*

['Once it was the colour of saying', *PDJ*, 144].

(iii) 'The revolving hill to my father's house reached to the sky', thinks young Thomas, returning home drunk.
['Old Garbo', *Portrait*, *CS*, 217].

(iv) In *Adventures in the Skin Trade* the Drive is thinly disguised as 'Mortimer Street'.

'Mortimer Street is what is right', 'writes' Samuel Bennet in the ironic letter he imagines sending to his mother.
['A Fine Beginning', *ST*, *CS*, 250. See also 'A Fine Beginning', *ST*, *CS*, 242, 246, 252, and 'Plenty of Furniture', *ST*, *CS*, 268, 271-2].

(v) First Voice remembers Thomas when a boy being chased through the fields behind the Drive.
['Return Journey', *CS*, 327].

(vi) 'the chilly glinting hill . . . the seaward hill'.
['A Child's Christmas in Wales', *CS*, 298, 301].

(vii) Where the day ends.
['Holiday Memory', *CS*, 310].

Map 4 (p. 78).

## 5 Cwmdonkin Drive

Thomas's birthplace: he was born in the front bedroom on 27 October 1914 and named Dylan Marlais Thomas.

No. 5 was his home until 10 November 1934, when he left to live for the first time in London. He came home for Christmas. Thereafter he lived at No. 5 during March 1935, early summer 1935, from October 1935 to January 1936 (except for one visit to London during November 1935), March 1936, and from June/July 1936 to February 1937 (intermittently).

In April 1937 his parents sold the house and moved to Bishopston.

Thomas's was the back bedroom next to the noisy boiler. There — and in his father's downstairs study — he read voraciously, filled the famous *Notebooks*, and wrote his first published poems.

*Letters:*
(i)   'my nasty, provincial address'.
      [*CL*, 20: to Pamela Hansford Johnson (mid-September 1933)].
(ii)  'a provincial villa'.
      [*CL*, 27: to Pamela Hansford Johnson (15 October 1933)].
(iii) 'a Glamorgan villa'.
      [*CL*, 43: to Pamela Hansford Johnson (early November 1933)].
(iv)  'a small, not very well painted, gateless house' . . . Very nice, very respectable'.
      [*CL*, 146: to Pamela Hansford Johnson (about 3 July 1934)].
(v)   'a mortgaged villa in an upper-class professional row'.
      [*CL*, 216: to Wyn Henderson (9 March 1936)].
*Works:*
(i)   'Leaning from windows over a
                     length of lawns,
      On tumbling hills admiring the
                                    sea'.
      ['Poet: 1935', *PDJ*, 48].
(ii)  Where the poet hears the wind and sees ships anchor in the bay.
      ['Ears in the turrets hear', *PDJ*, 62].
(iii) Where young Thomas cannot face his Sunday lunch after a night out with Mr Farr.
      ['Old Garbo', *Portrait*, *CS*, 217].
(iv)  'Lavengro', where the story takes place, is partly based on No. 5.
      ['Where Tawe Flows', *Portrait*, *CS*, 181-95].
      See also, *69 Glanbrydan Avenue*, below.
(v)   Where the small boy plays before being taken to the park.
      ['Patricia, Edith, and Arnold', *Portrait*, *CS*, 144-6].
(vi)  As Samuel Bennet's home in 'Mortimer Street' No. 5 is described in some detail.
      ['A Fine Beginning', *ST*, *CS*, 239-46].
(vii) The setting.
      ['A Child's Christmas in Wales', *CS*, 296-303].
**Map 4 (p. 78).**

*No. 5 Cwmdonkin Drive in 1986*

34

*Cwmdonkin Park*

*Cwmdonkin Park*

As a boy and as an adolescent Thomas was often found here. The Park was one of his most important places.

In his time part was a reservoir but this, the bandstand, and the hunchback, have long gone. The fountain survives (though a push-button tap has replaced the chained drinking-cups) as do the bowling-club's shelter and storeroom. A bell is still rung at closing-time.

Since 1963 a memorial to Thomas has stood near the Park's main entrance: on a block of local stone are carved the last three lines of 'Fern Hill'. A memorial shelter is near the old bandstand.

*Letters:*

(i)   The park is in Thomas's list of Swansea's main features.
      [*CL*, 146: to Pamela Hansford Johnson (about 3 July 1934)].

(ii)  Thoughts of Cwmdonkin Park made him homesick, Thomas writes from Ireland.
      [*CL*, 191: to Bert Trick (Summer 1935)].

(iii) 'I wish we were there now', he writes from Oxford.
      [*CL*, 588 (27 April 1946)].

*Works:*

(i)   The setting of the poem.
      ['Rain cuts the place we tread', *PDJ*, 13-14; *Notebooks*, 107-8].

(ii)  The setting of parts of the poem.
      ['Poet: 1935', *PDJ*, 46-8; *Notebooks*, 177-80].

(iii) 'I sit and mark
      Love wet its arrow in the park'.
      ['Not from this anger, anticlimax after', *Notebooks*, 192; deleted from *PDJ*, 134)].

(iv)  An important part of his early life.

['The first ten years in school and park', *Notebooks*, 193].

(v)   'the star-gestured children in the park'.
      ['Especially when the October wind', *PDJ*, 98; *Notebooks*, 348].

(vi)  'The ball I threw while playing in the park
      Has not yet reached the ground'.
      ['Should lanterns shine', *PDJ*, 116].

(vii) '. . . I whistled with mitching boys
                through a reservoir park
      . . . and stoned the cold and
                cuckoo Lovers'.
      ['Once it was the colour of saying', *PDJ*, 144].

(viii) Where young Thomas, in a state of post-prandial fragility, goes to feel sorry for himself.
      ['Old Garbo', *Portrait*, *CS*, 217].

(ix)  Thomas, camping at Rhossilli, thinks of life continuing in Cwmdonkin and its park.
      ['Extraordinary Little Dogs', *Portrait*, *CS*, 168].

(x)   (a) The narrator lives near the park.
      (b) During some nights Tom sits in the park listening to the owls.
      ['Just Like Little Dogs', *Portrait*, *CS*, 177].

(xi)  Where Patricia and Edith meet Arnold.
      ['Patricia, Edith, and Arnold', *Portrait*, *CS*, 146-52].

(xii) The park could be seen as the main subject of one of Thomas's most famous poems.
      ['The Hunchback in the park', *PDJ*, 171-2; *Notebooks*, 155-6. 297-8].

(xiii) 'a world within the world of the sea town . . . full of terrors and treasures . . . a country just born and always changing'.

['Reminiscences of Childhood (Second Version)', *QEOM*, 9].

(xiv) The Narrator hears 'the childish, lonely, remembered music fingering on in the suddenly gentle wind'.

['Return Journey', *CS*, 328].

Map 4 (p. 78).

## Cwmdonkin Terrace

Where young Thomas and his friends would ring doorbells.

['Reminiscences of Childhood (Second Version), *QEOM*, 10].

Map 4 (p. 78).

## Dan Lewis's

Unidentified. Thomas refers to it as a town-centre boot-shop.

Where Leslie Bird worked.

['Old Garbo', *Portrait*, *CS*, 208].

## 29 Delhi Street, St Thomas

Birthplace (1882) of Thomas's mother, Florence Hannah Williams. When she met D. J. Thomas she was a seamstress in a local drapers. St Thomas was, and remains, a working-class area close to the Docks.

Map 7 (p. 81).

## Dirty Black's, Union Street

No longer in existence. 'Dirty Black's, the Fancy Man' was a shop selling jokes, novelties and contraceptives (hence the nickname).

Young Thomas stares at the window but does not dare to go inside in case a woman serves him.

['Old Garbo', *Portrait*, *CS*, 211].

Map 3 (p. 77).

*29 Delhi Street, St Thomas, in 1986*

## Docks

These are still important but, in Thomas's day, they were a dominant presence in the town.

*Letter:*

A romantically suicidal Thomas occasionally thought of throwing himself in.

[*CL*, 127: to Pamela Hansford Johnson (2 May 1934)].

*Works:*

(i) Mr O'Brien drives Lou and the young man past the 'still droning docks' on their way to Lou's room.

['One Warm Saturday', *Portrait*, *CS*, 231].

(ii) Mr Farr and young Thomas pub-crawl partly through windy, sleazy dockland.

['Old Garbo', *Portrait*, *CS*, 216 &

*Ebenezer Chapel in 1985*

*passim*].

(iii) As the young men stand in Trafalgar Arch the Docks seem to disappear. ['Just Like Little Dogs', *Portrait, CS*, 176].

(iv) (a) Idlers watch the ships sailing in and out.
(b) The boy looks down on the docks as he flies over the town.
['Reminiscences of Childhood (Second Version)', *QEOM*, 8, 14].

(v) 'the sun-dazed docks round the corner of the sand-hills . . . the calling docks'.
['Holiday Memory', *CS*, 307-8].

(vi) (a) The Narrator's first impression of Swansea is of the cold wind from the docks.
(b) The Promenade-Man remembers the young boy watching the ships.
['Return Journey', *CS*, 316, 326].

(vii) Thomas recalls the sounds of the sea-gulls from the docks.
['A Child's Christmas in Wales', *CS*, 302].

Map 7 (p. 81).

*Ebenezer Baptist Chapel, Ebenezer Street*
The Narrator walks at night through the streets near 'ghostly Ebenezer'.
['Just Like Little Dogs', *Portrait, CS*, 177].
Map 3 (p. 77).

*Elysium Cinema, High Street*
Mentioned by the barmaid.
['Return Journey', *CS*, 316].
Map 3 (p. 77).

*Empire Theatre, Oxford Street*
This was once Swansea's main theatre. It was next to the old Carlton Cinema building in Oxford Street before being demolished and replaced by a super-market.

*Letter:*
Thomas recalls hearing opera there.
[*CL*, 455 (c. 5 June 1940)].

*Works:*
(i) 'I've seen over twenty chorines from the Empire . . . drunk as printers', says the barman.
['One Warm Saturday', *Portrait, CS*, 224].

(ii) Young Thomas, killing time before meeting Mr Farr, watches the theatre queue, scans the posters, and thinks about the chorus girls.
['Old Garbo', *Portrait, CS*, 211].

Map 3 (p. 77).

*Esplanade*
See *Promenade*, below.

*Evening Post Offices, Castle Street*
From 1931 to 1932, immediately after leaving school, Thomas worked as a junior reporter for the *South Wales Daily Post* (it became the *South Wales Evening Post* shortly after he joined).

(i) Where the story begins.
['Old Garbo', *Portrait, CS*, 206-10].

(ii) Outside the offices adjacent to the Castle, to which the *Evening Post* moved after the war, the Narrator asks Passers-by if he remembers Thomas as a journalist.
['Return Journey', *CS*, 321].

Map 1 (p. 18).

*38 Eversley Road, Sketty*
Here, in a house that is still called 'Warmley', lived Daniel Jones, Thomas's

closest friend. Thomas was a frequent visitor.

*Letters:*
(i) 'I still feel Warmley', writes Thomas from Hampshire.
[*CL*, 352: to Charles Fisher (January 1939)].
(ii) 'I feel very Warmley to him all the time', Thomas writes about Daniel Jones.
[*CL*, 518 (27 July 1941)].
(iii) Thomas doesn't wish to visit 'adanabandoned Swansea'.
[*CL*, 910: to Daniel Jones (24 August 1953)].

*Works:*
(a) The setting of most of the story, in which the Jones family is renamed 'Jenkyn'. Daniel Jones's middle name was 'Jenkyn'.
(b) As Mr Jenkyn talks to a neighbour outside the house he looks as if he is 'trying to swim down Eversley Road'.
(c) The story ends with the two boys running down Eversley Road before parting at the corner.
['The Fight', *Portrait*, *CS*, 153-64, 158, 164].
Map 5 (p. 79).

*Eynon's*
This local baker and pastrycook had — and has — numerous shops.
The narrator imagines buying fancy cakes.
['The Fight', *Portrait*, *CS*, 158].

*Fairground, Mumbles Road*
To which the family go after their afternoon on the beach.

*38 Eversley Road ('Warmley') in 1986*

['Holiday Memory',*CS*, 308].
Map 2 (p. 76).

*Fishguard Alley*
Near the '*Fishguard Arms*' (see below).
'where the methylated-spirit drinkers danced into the policemen's arms'.
['Just Like Little Dogs', *Portrait*, *CS*, 174].
Map 1 (p. 18).

*Fishguard Arms, 28 Strand*
This pub no longer exists.
It is visited by young Thomas and Mr Farr: 'you can see the sailors knitting there in the public bar'.
['Old Garbo', *Portrait*, *CS*, 207, 212, 213-18].
Map 1 (p. 18).

*69 Glanbrydan Avenue in 1986*

*Fullers Row, Mount Pleasant*
Seen by the Narrator as he stands in bombed High Street.
['Return Journey', *CS*, 316].
Map 3 (p. 77).

*Gasworks, Oystermouth Road*
'impressive'.
['Reminiscences of Childhood (Second Version)', *QEOM*, 12].
Map 3 (p. 77).

*69 Glanbrydan Avenue*
Once the home and shop of Bert Trick, the communist grocer, a close friend and mentor of Thomas's. Thomas and friends met for informal discussion in the living-room behind the shop. Here Trick's infant daughter Pamela asked the question, 'What colour is glory?', that appears in early versions of 'Why east wind chills' (*Notebooks*, 204-6) and in 'My World is Pyramid' (*PDJ*, 104).
The Narrator walks past on his way to the Uplands and remembers eating and talking there.
['Return Journey', *CS*, 326].
Map 4 (p. 78).

*Goat Street*
Destroyed by bombs.
(i)  Young Thomas and Mr Farr walk through Goat Street to the Carlton Hotel. The youth notices women in men's caps standing in doorways.

*Grammar School, Mount Pleasant*

['Old Garbo', *Portrait*, *CS*, 212].
(ii) 'where all the women wear men's caps'.
['Reminiscences of Childhood (Second Version)', *QEOM*, 14].
Map 1 (p. 18).

*Gorse Terrace*
Demolished. Trevor Hughes lived here, Thomas's close friend and the original of Raymond Price in 'Who Do You Wish Was With Us?'

*Gower Street*
Destroyed by bombs.
The Narrator walks through it on his way to the sea-shore.
['Return Journey', *CS*, 325].
Map 1 (p. 18).

*Grammar School, Mount Pleasant*
Bombed. After the war the school removed to De La Beche Road, Sketty, as Bishop Gore School.

Thomas's father, D. J. Thomas, was senior English master. Thomas attended 1925-31. He contributed to and eventually edited the school magazine, had some success at athletics and acted in school plays. He passed no examinations except for English.
*Letters:*
(i) Where, he says, he first encountered

alcohol.
[*CL*, 43: to Pamela Hansford Johnson (early November 1933)].
(ii) 'where I did no work at all'.
[*CL*, 98: to Glyn Jones (c. 14 March 1934)].

*Works:*
(i) 'content, and "Be content"
Ring like a handbell through the corridors.'
['Why east wind chills', *PDJ*, 56].
(ii) (a) Where Thomas and Dan Jenkyn fight, and Thomas shows off his black eye.
(b) Where the drawing class studies female anatomy — and talks.
['The Fight', *Portrait, CS*, 153-5].
(iii) 'the School on Mount Pleasant Hill has changed its face and its ways', laments the Narrator in the bombed building.
['Return Journey', *CS*, 324].
(iv) In the lower forms, Shakespeare was 'heard, read, and near-murdered'.
['Poetic Manifesto', *EP*, 157].
Map 3 (p. 77).

### Griffiths & Sons, 31-4 Castle Street
An outfitters no longer in existence.
Young Thomas and his mother look at the window display.
['The Fight', *Portrait, CS*, 159].
Map 1 (p. 18).

### The Grove, Uplands
A leafy square close to Cwmdonkin Drive and the Park.
(i) Thinly disguised as 'snoring Stanley's Grove'.
['A Fine Beginning', *ST, CS*, 243; see also, 'A Fine Beginning', *ST, CS*, 242, 246, 249, and 'Plenty of Furniture',

*ST, CS*, 272].
(ii) The Narrator walks through it into the Park. No. 47 was Mrs Ferguson's sweet-shop.
['Return Journey', *CS*, 327, 328].
Map 4 (p. 78).

### Hafod
A working-class area near the north end of High Street.
In High Street, recalls Thomas the young journalist, 'sirens from the Hafod sat in the steaming chip shops with their hand-bags on their knees and their ear-rings rattling'.
['Old Garbo', *Portrait, CS*, 211].

### Hanover Street
'tell us about Mrs Pussie Edwards in Han-over Street', the Grammar School boys beg Cyril.
['The Fight', *Portrait, CS*, 155].
Map 4 (p. 78).

### Harbour Trust Offices, Adelaide Street
Dead Mr Baxter, whose widow was the Bennet's next-door neighbour in Mortimer Street, once worked here.
['A Fine Beginning', *ST, CS*, 242].
Map 3 (p. 77).

### Heart's Delight
Unidentified, but seemingly in the St Thomas area (see *New Cut Bridge*, below).
Where Mrs Prothero spent all the collection money.
['Old Garbo', *Portrait, CS*, 217].

### Helen's Road
See *St Helen's Road*, below.

*Harbour Trust Offices*

## High Street

Now in decline but, in Thomas's day, this was Swansea's main street.

(i) (a) Where parts of the story take place.

(b) Where Thomas goes to drink coffee with his friends at the Café Royal.

(c) As he waits for Mr Farr he thinks romantically of his 'dead youth in the vanished High Street nights'.

['Old Garbo', *Portrait, CS,* 211, 207–212].

(ii) (a) The High Street billiards saloon insisted on correct dress.

(b) Young Thomas sometimes walked through 'dead and empty High Street under the moon'.

['Just Like Little Dogs', *Portrait, CS,* 175, 177].

(iii) Raymond Price says he wouldn't change Gower for High Street.

['Who Do You Wish Was With Us?' *Portrait, CS,* 199].

(iv) Where young Thomas wishes to escape his embarrassing mother.

['The Fight', *Portrait, CS,* 159].

(v) (a) Where the Narrator begins his journey.

(b) He lists some of the bombed shops: Eddershaw's, Curry's, Donegal Clothing Company, Doctor

*High Street in 1937*

Scholl's, Burton's, W. H. Smith, Boots, Leslie's Stores, Upson's Shoes, Prince of Wales Hotel, Tucker's Fish, Stead & Simpson, and Hodges Clothiers.
['Return Journey', *CS*, 316, 319].
Map 1 (p. 18) & Map 3 (p. 77).

### High Street Arcade
Demolished. Its main shop was Snell's Music.
Young Thomas decides against going the long way back to the *Evening Post* office: from High Street to Castle Street via the Arcade.
['Old Garbo', *Portrait*, *CS*, 209].
Map 1 (p. 18).

### High Street Railway Station
Then Great Western Railway; now British Rail and Swansea's only surviving station. Here Thomas caught trains to London.
[*CL*, 145: to Pamela Hansford Johnson (about 3 July 1934)].
Map 3 (p. 77).

### Hospital, St Helen's Road
Now closed and redeveloped.
Where Thomas, the young reporter, called.
['Return Journey', *CS*, 321].
Map 4 (p. 78).

*High Street Station*

*Inkerman Street, St Thomas*
One of the streets adjoining Delhi Street (where Thomas's mother was born and relations still lived).
(i)  Glimpsed by the flying boy.
     ['Reminiscences of Childhood (Second Version)', *QEOM*, 14].
(ii) Where Leslie and the narrator follow Hermione. In this story, in a rare instance of blurred topography, Inkerman Street is placed near the town-centre.
     ['The Followers', *CS*, 333].
Map 7 (p. 81).

*International Stores, High Street*
Unidentified. There were, then, no such grocers in Swansea. Probably Thomas meant the 'Home and Colonial' in High Street, or — possibly and satirically —

'John Bull' stores.
      The young men drinking coffee in the Café Royal watch the shop-girls across the street.
['Old Garbo', *Portrait*, *CS*, 208].
Map 1 (p. 18) & Map 3 (p. 77).

*Italian Chip Shop, High Street*
Probably Adrio's, 109 High Street — now gone.
      The young reporter walks past into Chapel Street.
['Old Garbo', *Portrait*, *CS*, 209].
Map 1 (p. 18).

*Jew's Harp Public House*
Not positively identified. This may have been the nickname of the 'Compass' Tavern (later the 'Nag's Head'), next to the Synagogue in Goat Street.

46

*Inkerman Street, St Thomas, in 1986*

Mrs Emerald Franklin is a regular. ['One Warm Saturday', *Portrait*, *CS*, 226]. Map 1 (p. 18).

### Kardomah Cafe, 14 Castle Street

Destroyed by bombs. This was Thomas's favourite place for coffee and chat with Daniel Jones, Alfred Janes, and others. See also, *Café Royal, above.*

*Letter:*

(i)  'my Home Sweet Homah'.
 [*CL*, 434: to Charles Fisher (December 1939)].

*Works:*

(i)  Outside which Thomas's mother waits to embarrass him.
 ['The Fight', *Portrait*, *CS*, 159].

(ii)  The Narrator recalls the destroyed Kardomah and the lost voices of 'poets, painters, and musicians in their beginnings'.
 ['Return Journey', *CS*, 322, 323].
Map 1 (p. 18).

### King's Arms, High Street

Near enough to the B.B.C. studios in Alexandra Road for Thomas to have a 'quick one' before broadcasting. [*CL*, 909: to Ralph Wishart (28 July 1953). Thomas — probably mistakenly — refers to the 'King's *Head*', which, pre-war, was across the town at 262 Oxford Street]. Map 3 (p. 77).

*Kitchener Street*
Unidentified; Swansea had no street of this name.
   Up which Leslie and the Narrator once followed an 'old girl'.
['The Followers', *CS*, 331].

*Little Theatre, Southend, Mumbles*
Thomas acted with Swansea Little Theatre in a small church-hall near the Mermaid and Antelope pubs. The association is commemorated in the Little Theatre's current — and permanent — address: 'The Dylan Thomas Theatre' in the Maritime Quarter.
Map 6 (p. 80).

*Llangyfelach*
'these names are as fearsome to me as they are to you'.
   He mis-spelled it 'Llangyfellach'.
[*CL*, 24: to Pamela Hansford Johnson (15 October 1933)].

*Llewellyn Hall, Y.M.C.A. Building, Page Street*
Where Thomas acted in Grammar School plays.
Map 3 (p. 77).

*Llwyn-y-Bryn High School for Girls, Walter Road*
The Girls' School in Stanley Road attended by Samuel Bennet's sister.
['A Fine Beginning', *ST*, *CS*, 241].
Map 4 (p. 78).

*Lord Jersey Inn, 3 Orange Street*
Destroyed by bombs.

Where Mr Farr and young Thomas drink during their pub-crawl; 'there's shilling women in the "Lord Jersey"', says Mr Farr.
['Old Garbo', *Portrait*, *CS*, 207. See also, 212, 215, 218].
Map 1 (p. 18).

*Lord Nelson Hotel, 14 Calvert Street*
Destroyed by bombs. Possibly the reference is to the 'Lord Nelson', 171 High Street; almost certainly Thomas meant Calvert Street.
   'Come and have one tonight in the "Nelson". There's a girl down there who'll show you where the sailor bit her.'
['Old Garbo', *Portrait*, *CS*, 218].
Map 1 (p. 18).

*Mackworth Hotel, High Street*
Demolished.
Where the Narrator begins his search for the young Dylan Thomas.
['Return Journey', *CS*, 316-19].
Map 1 (p. 18).

*Majestic*
Unidentified.
A night there is recalled by one of the young men in the Trafalgar Arch.
['Just Like Little Dogs', *Portrait*, *CS*, 176].

*Mannesmann Hall, Plasmarl*
Demolished. Its site is now Mannesmann Road, off the Plasmarl By-Pass. The hall was an important venue for boxing matches.
(i)   Where the other young man should be.

*Mackworth Hotel*

['Just Like Little Dogs', *Portrait*, *CS*, 175].

(ii)  Where young Thomas showed little understanding of boxing.
['Return Journey', *CS*, 320].

*Manselton*
A residential working-class area north of the city centre.
Where lived Daphne, the grass-widow for whom Mr Roberts had lost his job and his reputation.
['Where Tawe Flows', *Portrait*, *CS*, 183-4].

*Marine Hotel, Mumbles Road*
A favourite of Thomas's.
Map 6 (p. 80).

*Maritime Quarter*
A statue of Dylan Thomas is in Dylan Thomas Square, near the Dylan Thomas Theatre. The poet sits in a wooden arm-chair; the chair is a fine likeness.
Map 3 (p. 77).

*Marks & Spencers's, Victoria Arcade*
(Goat Street to Waterloo Street)
'She looked like a bit of Marks and Spencer's', says Leslie, scornfully, of a girl he knew.
['Old Garbo', *Portrait*, *CS*, 208].
Map 1 (p. 18).

*Marlborough Hotel*
Unidentified; Swansea had no public house of this name.

Where Leslie and the Narrator stop for a drink.
['The Followers', CS, 330, 331, 334].

*Melba Pavilion*
See *Patti Pavilion*, below.

*Mermaid Hotel, Mumbles Road, Mumbles*
Always a favourite Thomas haunt.
*Letters:*
(i)  'Muse or Mermaid?' wonders 18-years-old Thomas.
     [CL, 7-8: to Trevor Hughes (February 1932)].
(ii) Thomas recounts an evening with Daniel Jones in 'the womb of the Mermaid'.

[CL, 161: to Trevor Hughes (prob. Summer 1934)].
(iii) Where he calls regularly.
      [CL, 85: to Pamela Hansford Johnson (prob. early January 1934)].
(iv) Thomas writes wistfully from Ireland of his 'Mumbles Mermaid (bless her hair and her tail)'.
      [CL, 191: to Bert Trick (prob. July 1935)].

*Works:*
(i)  Salnady creeps up the stairs of the 'Mermaid' for an illegal Sunday drink with the manageress.
     ['Spajma and Salnady', EP, 144-5].
(ii) Where young Thomas broke his front tooth.
     ['Return Journey', CS, 318].
Map 6 (p. 80).

*Mermaid Hotel in late 1970s*

*Metropole Hotel, Wind Street*
Demolished.
Where young journalist Thomas attended an auction.
['Return Journey', *CS*, 321].
Map 3 (p. 77).

*Milton Terrace, Mount Pleasant*
Seen by the Narrator as he stands in bombed High Street.
['Return Journey', *CS*, 316].
Map 3 (p. 77).

*22 Mirador Crescent, Uplands*
Mrs Hole's private school which Thomas attended before entering Swansea Grammar School.
*Letter:*
**Where he first smoked cigarettes.**

*22 Mirador Crescent in 1986*

[*CL*, 43: to Pamela Hansford Johnson (early November 1933)].
*Works:*
(i)   An important part of his childhood.
      ['The first ten years in school and park', *Notebooks*, 193].
(ii)  'so firm and kind and smelling of goloshes'.
      ['Reminiscences of Childhood (Second Version), *QEOM*, 13].
(iii) Described by First Voice.
      ['Return Journey', *CS*, 327].
Map 4 (p. 78).

*Mirador Lane, Uplands*
The 'lane of confidences' that ran behind Mirador Crescent and Thomas's first school.
['Reminiscences of Childhood (Second Version)', *QEOM*, 13-14].
Map 4 (p. 78).

*Missions to Seamen Institute, Harbour Road*
'There might be a quarrel with razors, and once Ted Williams found a lip outside the Mission to Seamen'.
['Old Garbo', *Portrait*, *CS*, 210].

*Modern Café*
Unidentified.
Where Mrs Constable has a cup of tea.
['Old Garbo', *Portrait*, *CS*, 208].

*Mortimer Street*
See *Cwmdonkin Drive*, above.

*Mortuary, 47 Arches, Strand*
Young journalists were obliged to call there regularly.

*Mirador Lane in 1986*

(i) (a) Young Thomas and Mr Farr walk past on their way to the 'Fishguard'.
(b) In the 'Fishguard' snuggery Thomas is introduced to Jack Stiff, the mortuary keeper.
['Old Garbo', *Portrait*, *CS*, 213-14].

(ii) The young narrator, loitering in Tra-falgar Arch, thinks of scavengers asleep in sidings or laid out 'beyond pickings on Jack Stiff's slab near the pub'.
['Just Like Little Dogs', *Portrait*, *CS*, 174].

(iii) 'He went pale green, mun', recalls the Old Reporter of Thomas's first sight of a corpse.
['Return Journey', *CS*, 320].

Map 3 (p. 77).

*Mount Pleasant Hill*

Where the Grammar School was.

(i) As Thomas reads his poetry to Dan Jenkyn the Grammar School seems to disappear into a deep hole on Mount Pleasant Hill.
['The Fight', *Portrait*, *CS*, 159].

(ii) The Narrator, standing in bombed High Street, sees the 'swathed hill stepping up out of the town'.
['Return Journey', *CS*, 316].

(iii) Where the Narrator finds the bombed school.
['Return Journey', *CS*, 324-5].

Map 3 (p. 77).

*Mount Pleasant Hospital*
See *Workhouse*, below.

*Mumbles*
A village-suburb at the western end of
Swansea Bay. It was — and is — a place of
pubs, fishing and sailing boats, general
amusements, a pier, and a lighthouse. The
*Little Theatre* (see above) was at Southend.
For Thomas the area effectively included
*Oystermouth* (see below) and Newton (see
*Paraclete Chapel*, below), where his Auntie
Dosie lived.

See also, *Antelope, Marine, Mermaid*,
above.

*Letters:*
(i)   A hung-over Thomas regrets
      'Mumbles and the oystered beer'.
      [*CL*, 161: to Trevor Hughes (prob.
      Summer 1934)].

(ii)  'a rather nice village, despite its
      name'.
      [*CL*, 85: to Pamela Hansford Johnson
      (prob. early January 1934)].

*Works:*
(i)   'Mumbles where the aunties grew'.
      ['Holiday Memory', *CS*, 307].
(ii)  The birthplace of 'Fourth Drowned
      . . . Alfred Pomeroy Jones'.
      [*UMW*, 4].

Map 6 (p. 80).

*Mumbles Head*
The Promenade-Man stares at it across
the bay.
['Return Journey', *CS*, 325].
Map 6 (p. 80).

*Mumbles Lighthouse*
(i)   Young Thomas imagines walking out

*Mumbles Pier and Lighthouse*

with the barmaid from the 'Three Lamps' to where 'couples lay loving under their coats and looking at the Mumbles lighthouse'.
['Old Garbo', *Portrait*, *CS*, 212].

(ii) The narrator, loitering in Trafalgar Arch, sees the 'lighthouse beams' from across the bay.
['Just Like Little Dogs', *Portrait*, *CS*, 175].
Map 6 (p. 80).

*Mumbles Pier*

(i) 'It's no good in the rain, is it?' complains the young narrator, in a discussion of where to loiter.
['Just Like Little Dogs', *Portrait*, *CS*, 176].

(ii) Thomas recalls visiting the 'gaunt pier . . . with . . . its skeleton legs'.
['Reminiscences of Childhood (Second Version)', *QEOM*, 13].
Map 6 (p. 80).

*Mumbles Road*

(i) The young man crosses it from the beach to 'Victoria Gardens' (Victoria Park).
['One Warm Saturday', *Portrait*, *CS*, 221].

(ii) Where, in the snow, Jim and young Thomas imagine themselves to be Arctic trappers.
['A Child's Christmas in Wales', *CS*, 296].
Map 2 (p. 76) & Map 6 (p. 80).

*Mumbles Road at Brynmill Lane in 1925*

*Museum ('Royal Institution of South Wales') in 1986*

*Museum, Victoria Road*
The Royal Institution of South Wales.
(i)   Mrs Franklin had been seen 'with a black man last Wednesday, round by the museum'.
['One Warm Saturday', *Portrait, CS*, 226].
(ii)  Where loose — and cheap — women could be found.
['Just Like Little Dogs', *Portrait, CS*, 177].
(iii) 'the museum that should have been in a museum'.
['Reminiscences of Childhood (Second Version)', *QEOM*, 12].
Map 3 (p. 77).

*New Cut Bridge, Quay Parade*
Over which Mrs Prothero walks to the 'Heart's Delight', and from which she jumps.
['Old Garbo', *Portrait, CS*, 217].
Map 3 (p. 77).

*Norfolk Street*
Where George Gray lived.
See also, *Sketty*, below.
['Who Do You Wish Was With Us?', *Portrait, CS*, 204].
Map 3 (p. 77).

*The 'No. 10' Public House in Union Street*

'No. 10', Union Street

A pub — still in existence — often used by Thomas. In 1940 he failed to meet Vernon Watkins there.

[*CL*, 454 (June 1940)].

Map 3 (p. 77).

*Paraclete Chapel in 1986*

*Old Red Cow Inn, 210 High Street*
Thomas used 'Red Cow' to name the pub
in Wilshire's picture.
[*The Beach of Falesá*, 41].
Map 3 (p. 77).


*Oystermouth*
'beery and fleshly'.
[*CL*, 191: to Bert Trick (prob. July 1935)].
Map 6 (p. 80).


*Paraclete Congregational Church, Newton
Road, Newton*
Thomas's Aunt Theodosia ('Dosie') was
married to the minister, Reverend David
Rees. As a small boy Thomas stayed with

them and attended the Sunday School.
Map 6 (p. 80).


*Paradise Alley*
See *Paradise Passage*, below.
Where Mrs Penelope Bogan lived.
['The Followers', *CS*, 330].
Map 3 (p. 77).


*Paradise Passage*
This and *Paradise Alley* are thin disguises
for Salubrious Passage and Place (today,
linking Wind Street and Princess Way).
  Through which Leslie and the narrator
follow Hermione.
['The Followers', *CS*, 333].
Map 3 (p. 77).

*'Paradise Passage' (Salubrious Passage, Wind Street)*

## Park Drive, Cwmdonkin
As Thomas walks to Sketty reciting aloud his voice sounds like a stranger in Park Drive.
['The Fight', *Portrait*, *CS*, 156].
Map 4 (p. 78).

## Patti Pavilion, Victoria Park
Always referred to by Thomas — jokingly — as *Melba Pavilion*. (Patti was Adelina Patti, the famous soprano, who once lived locally and gave the pavilion to the town. Hence 'Melba', after the equally famous soprano, Nellie Melba.)

(i) Where Leslie suggests they go dancing.
['Old Garbo', *Portrait*, *CS*, 209].
(ii) Walter tells what went on in the ladies' cloakroom during a concert.
['Just Like Little Dogs', *Portrait*, *CS*, 178].
(iii) If in possession of a million pounds the Grammar School class would buy a huge house with a luxurious lavatory as big as the Melba Pavilion.
['The Fight', *Portrait*, *CS*, 155].
Map 4 (p. 78).

## Plaza Cinema, Picton Place
Demolished and redeveloped as the Odeon Cinema and Tesco Supermarket, Kingsway.
Thomas, the young journalist, gets in free and watches a romantic American film.
['Old Garbo', *Portrait*, *CS*, 210-11].
Map 3 (p. 77).

## Prince of Wales Hotel, 6 High Street
Destroyed by bombs.
['Return Journey', *CS*, 316].
Map 3 (p. 77).

## Promenade, Mumbles Road
In Thomas's day a popular walk and a place to meet girls.
(i) (a) Where Leslie picked-up a nurse.
(b) Where young Thomas imagines walking with the barmaid from the 'Three Lamps'.
['Old Garbo', *Portrait*, *CS*, 208, 212].
(ii) The railway-arches were not far-off.
['Just Like Little Dogs', *Portrait*, *CS*, 175].
(iii) Where Samuel Bennet met the man

who gave him Lucille Harris's address.
['A Fine Beginning', *ST*, *CS*, 247].
(iv) (a) Where the Narrator meets the Promenade-Man.
(b) Where young Thomas picks-up Hetty Harris's friend.
['Return Journey', *CS*, 325-6].
Map 2 (p. 76).


*Rabbaiotti's Café, 33 High Street*
(i) Where girls could be found.
['Just Like Little Dogs', *Portrait*, *CS*, 175].
(ii) The young men stop outside the café after running away from Dulcie.
['The Followers', *CS*, 333].
Map 3 (p. 77).


*Railway Line, Swansea Bay*
The old L.M.S. line (now gone) from Victoria Station around part of Swansea Bay.
(i) The young man crosses 'the useless railway covered with sand' on his way from the beach to 'Victoria Gardens' (Victoria Park).
['One Warm Saturday', *Portrait*, *CS*, 223. See also, 221].
(ii) Along which trains run noisily during the family's afternoon on the beach.
['Holiday Memory', *CS*, 307].


*Recreation Ground, Mumbles Road*
Where Thomas and his friends played cricket on the 'bald and cindery surface'.
['Reminiscences of Childhood (Second Version)' *QEOM*, 13].
Map 2 (p. 76).

*The Regal Cinema, Newton Road, Oystermouth*
Now a shopping arcade.
Where Thomas had recently seen an actress in a foam-bath.
['Old Garbo', *Portrait*, *CS*, 208].
Map 6 (p. 80).

*17 Richmond Road, Cwmdonkin, in 1986*

*17 Richmond Road, Cwmdonkin*
Home of the Grant-Murrays. Thomas played with his friends on an open space behind the house. There they built their Guy Fawkes bonfires.
Map 4 (p. 78).


*The Rising Sun*
Unidentified.
Where the murderer shows the bloody

vest.
['The Vest', CS, 34].

*Rodney Street, St Helen's*
The young man in the railway arch should have 'kids to bounce in a kitchen in Rodney Street'.
['Just Like Little Dogs', *Portrait*, CS, 175].
Map 4 (p. 78).

*St Augustus Crescent*
See *St Helen's Crescent*, below.

*St Helen's Avenue*
Probably.
Hermione lives at No. 13 ('Beach View').
['The Followers', CS, 125, 333, 336].
Map 4 (p. 78).

*St Helen's Crescent*
Almost certainly the 'St Augustus Crescent' through which Leslie and the Narrator follow Hermione. In this story the topography is unusually blurred.
['The Followers', CS, 333, 336].
Map 4 (p. 78).

*St Helen's Cricket Ground,*
*Mumbles Road*
Where Thomas often went 'to sit in the sun and watch a county cricket match'.
[CL, 160: to Pamela Hansford Johnson (20 July 1934)].
Map 4 (p. 78).

*St Helen's Road*
The Narrator goes down to the seashore 'along long Helen's Road'.
['Return Journey', CS, 325].
Map 4 (p. 78).

*St Mary's Church, St Mary's Square*
Bombed but rebuilt.
The hung-over Thomas is troubled by the bells.
['Old Garbo', *Portrait*, CS, 217].
Map 3 (p. 77).

*St Thomas*
A working-class area near the Docks on Swansea's east side where relations of Thomas still lived.
See *Delhi Street, St Thomas*, above.
(i)   George Hooping sometimes stayed in St Thomas 'with an aunt who could see through the walls'.
      ['Extraordinary Little Cough', *Portrait*, CS, 166].
(ii)  Part of the loitering young man's world.
      ['Just Like Little Dogs', *Portrait*, CS, 177].
Map 7 (p. 81).

*St Thomas's Church, Delhi Street*
The spire, from the landward side, is silhouetted against the cranes and gantries of Swansea Docks. According to Thomas's friend Ralph Wishart this was the inspiration of Thomas's poem, 'The Spire Cranes'. In the poem, it should be noted, the 'cranes' appear to be birds.
Map 7 (p. 81).

*Sandbanks*
A name used by Thomas for the *Sandfields* area.
See next entry.

*Sandfields*
In Thomas's time a poor area mainly between Oystermouth Road and the

Swansea Sands and Trafalgar Terrace.

*Sands (Swansea Bay)*

sands. Much was where the new County Hall now stands.

(i) When Thomas returns home with his black eye he is admonished for being 'as bad as a boy from the Sandbanks'. ['The Fight', *Portrait, CS*, 154].

(ii) Sandfields boys 'beachcombed, idled, and paddled'. ['Reminiscences of Childhood (Second Version)', *QEOM*, 8].

Map 3 (p. 77).

## Sands

The beach from the Docks to Mumbles. In pre-war days the stretch of sand nearest the town — known as 'the Slip' — was a popular pleasure-beach. The dunes, towards the middle of the bay, continue to attract courting couples.

(i) (a) Where the story begins. The young man wanders across the crowded beach opposite Trafalgar Terrace, then stares at it from the 'Victoria Saloon' (the 'Bay View Hotel').

(b) 'If you go for a constitutional after stop-tap along the sands you might as well be in Sodom and Gomorrah', Mrs Franklin tells her fellow-drinkers. ['One Warm Saturday', *Portrait, CS*, 219-21, 223, 226].

(ii) (a) Young Thomas imagines amorous adventures on the sands with the barmaid from the 'Three Lamps'.

(b) After drinking rum with Mr Farr young Thomas feels capable of rolling the 'Carlton' barmaid along the sands.

['Old Garbo', *Portrait*, *CS*, 212, 214].

(iii) (a) The narrator, loitering under Trafalgar Arch, stares out on 'miles of sands, long and dirty in the early dark'.

(b) He thinks of a stranger on the nearby sands listening to Tom and Walter's tale of adventures in the dunes with Dora and Norma.

['Just Like Little Dogs', *Portrait*, *CS*, 174, 178].

(iv) (a) Thomas recalls 'the bent and Devon-facing seashore', and the sands in summer.

(b) The flying boy glides over the sands and out to sea.

['Reminiscences of Childhood (Second Version)', *QEOM*, 12, 14].

(v) August Bank Holiday on the sands is the essay's main subject.

['Holiday Memory', *CS*, 304-10].

(vi) Thomas and friends walk the snowy beach on a Christmas afternoon.

['A Child's Christmas in Wales', *CS*, 301-2].

(vii) Where the Promenade-Man and young Thomas spent much of their time.

['Return Journey', *CS*, 325-6].

*Sebastapol Street, St Thomas*

(i) 'Katie Sebastopol Street' sings the national anthem in 'The Lord Jersey'.

*Singleton Hotel in 1986*

['Old Garbo', *Portrait*, *CS*, 215].

(ii) One of the streets over which the boy flies.
['Reminiscences of Childhood (Second Version)', *QEOM*, 14].
Map 7 (p. 81).

*Singleton Hotel, Singleton Street*
During the 1930s this pub was kept by Mrs Giles with whom Thomas, the young reporter, had lunch.
['Return Journey', *CS*, 321].
Map 3 (p. 77).

*Singleton Park, Sketty*
'crowded with lovers messing about'.
['The Fight', *Portrait*, *CS*, 159].
Map 5 (p. 79).

*Sketty*
Residential suburb in west Swansea where Daniel Jones lived in *Eversley Road*.

George Gray goes 'to somewhere in Sketty every morning to help a woman put her clothes on'.
['Who Do You Wish Was With Us?', *Portrait*, *CS*, 204].
Map 5 (p. 79).

*Sketty Church (St Paul's), Gower Road*
'Sketty church was shaking its bells for me', records young Thomas of his walk to Daniel Jenkyn's home.
['The Fight', *Portrait*, *CS*, 157].
Map 5 (p. 79).

*Singleton Park*

*Sketty Church and Gower Road in 1929*

### Sketty Green
Mrs Bertie Perkins lived at 'Rhydyrhelig' (now demolished). In July 1933 Thomas watched and subsequently wrote about an open-air performance of Sophocles' *Electra* given in her garden by Swansea Little Theatre.
(i)   Impressions of the performance.
      ['Greek Play in a Garden', *PDJ*, 56-7; *Notebooks*, 208-9].
(ii)  The Narrator recalls the poem's publication.
      ['Return Journey', *CS*, 318].
Map 5 (p. 79).

### Sketty Road
Along which go Thomas and Raymond Price as they hike from Uplands to Rhossilli.
['Who Do You Wish Was With Us?', *Portrait, CS*, 196].
Map 5 (p. 79).

### Slaughter-House, Dyfatty Street
Demolished.
(i)   (a) Where Mr Roberts used to smoke.
      (b) Mr Evans recalls the caretaker.
      ['Where Tawe Flows', *Portrait, CS*, 182-3].
(ii)  Young Thomas and friends used to wander past.

64

['Reminiscences of Childhood (Second Version)', *QEOM*, 12].
Map 3 (p. 77).

*Stanley Grove*
See *The Grove, Uplands*, above.

*Stanley Road*
See *Walter Road*, below.

*Strand*
Before World War Two this was one of Swansea's worst areas: slums, sleazy pubs, prostitutes, and dockland industry. It was partly bombed, has been much cleared and redeveloped, and is no longer residential.
    See also, *Fishguard Alley, Fishguard Arms, Mortuary*, above.
(a)  Thomas the young journalist goes back to the office via a 'short cut' near 'a slum called the Strand'.
(b)  His night out with Mr Farr is spent partly in Strand pubs: 'We crawled down Strand alleys by the side of the mortuary'.
    ['Old Garbo', *Portrait, CS*, 209, 213].
Map 3 (p. 77).

*Swansea Bay*
See also, *Sands*, above.
(i)  Boats in the bay are heard from outside the 'Fishguard Arms'.
    ['Old Garbo', *Portrait, CS*, 216].
(ii)  As Thomas reads his poems to his new friend, Dan Jenkyn, the noises of the town recede across the bay.
    ['The Fight', *Portrait, CS*, 159].
(iii)  Holiday-makers hear a motor-boat

*Strand (lower end) in 1928*

*A Strand alley*

out in the bay.
['Holiday Memory',*CS*, 307].

(iv) Ships sound out in the 'whirling bay' as young Thomas and friends walk home from the snowy beach.
['A Child's Christmas in Wales', *CS*, 302].

(v) The Promenade-Man and his dog stare across the bay as he remembers young Thomas watching the ships or listening to the foghorns.
['Return Journey', *CS*, 325-6].

(vi) Leslie and the narrator hear 'a ship hoot like a fog-ditched owl in the bay'.
['The Followers', *CS*, 330].

Map 2 (p. 76).

*Swansea Town Association Football Club, Vetch Field*

Now 'Swansea City A.F.C.', the local soccer club is still called 'the Swans'.

(i) Young Thomas and his new friend, Daniel Jenkyn, discuss whether 'the Swans' will beat 'Spurs'.
['The Fight', *Portrait*, *CS*, 158].

(ii) 'Ever seen young Thomas covering a soccer match down the Vetch and working it out in tries?' mocks the First Young Reporter.
['Return Journey', *CS*, 320].

Map 3 (p. 77).

*Tawe River*

(i) From which the story's title is

*Temple Street (and 'The Three Lamps') after the air-raids of 1941*

derived. The title refers to the novel, *Where Tawe Flows*, on which Thomas and his friends are collaborating.
['Where Tawe Flows', *Portrait*, *CS*, 181, 186, 187].
(ii) The beer is like 'half-frozen Tawe water'.
['Return Journey', *CS*, 316].
Map 7 (p. 81).

*Tawe Sands*
See *Sands*, above.

*Temple Street*
Destroyed by bombs.
Where the Narrator searches for the

'Three Lamps' hotel.
['Return Journey', *CS*, 319].
Map 1 (p. 18).

*Terrace Road*
Along which Thomas walked to the Grammar School.
(i) Young Thomas sees clouds sailing above it.
['The Fight', *Portrait*, *CS*, 154].
(ii) Thomas and friends discuss possible reactions to seeing a hippopotamus in Terrace Road.
['Memories of Christmas', *QEOM*, 25].
(iii) 'I seen you going to school along Terrace Road, Mr Glad-Eye, with

your little satchel and wearing your red cap', jeers Hetty Harris's friend on the Promenade.
['Return Journey', *CS*, 326].
Map 4 (p. 78).

*The Three Lamps Hotel, Temple Street*
Destroyed by bombs and rebuilt in Castle Gardens. A favourite pub of Thomas's.
(i)  Where young Thomas meets Mr Farr to begin their pub-crawl.
['Old Garbo', *Portrait*, *CS*, 210, 211-12].
(ii)  A regular in the 'Mackworth' remembers Thomas in the 'Three Lamps' 'lifting his ikkle elbow'.
['Return Journey', *CS*, 319].
Map 1 (p. 18).

*Tontine Street*
(i)  The young man is infatuated with Lou, even though 'she's no lady, with her sing-song Tontine voice'.
['One Warm Saturday', *Portrait*, *CS*, 228].
(ii)  Where Thomas the young reporter covers a chimney fire.
['Return Journey', *CS*, 321].
Map 3 (p. 77).

*Town Hill*
On the Cwmdonkin side of which (the 'Graig') Thomas played cowboys and Indians.
['Return Journey', *CS*, 327].

*Trafalgar Arch in 1986*

*Trafalgar Arch, Oystermouth Road*
The arch under the railway opposite what was Trafalgar Terrace and is now the stretch of Oystermouth Road adjacent to the 'Bay View Hotel'.

Where the narrator, Tom, and Walter loiter and talk. Thus, where the story takes place.
['Just Like Little Dogs', *Portrait*, *CS*, 174–80].
Map 4 (p. 78).

*Trafalgar Terrace, Oystermouth Road*
See *Trafalgar Arch*, above.
Which the narrator crosses on his way home from the Trafalgar Arch.
['Just Like Little Dogs', *Portrait*, *CS*, 180].
Map 2 (p. 76).

*Training College, Townhill Road*
Now part of the West Glamorgan Institute of Higher Education. Its grounds are close to Cwmdonkin Park.
(i) Young Thomas, off to camp at Rhossilli, hears tales of girls from the training college sunbathing naked on the rocks.
['Extraordinary Little Cough', *Portrait*, *CS*, 165].
(ii) As snow falls in the Park the training college is hidden by clouds.
['Patricia, Edith, and Arnold', *Portrait*, *CS*, 147].
Map 3 (p. 77).

*Union Street*
Where the story begins: young Thomas, waiting for his Uncle Jim outside a Union

*Training College from Cwmdonkin Park*

Street pub, imagines 'a man with spring-heeled boots and a two-edged knife . . . bouncing towards me from Union Street'. ['The Peaches', *Portrait*, CS, 123]. Map 3 (p. 77).

## University College of Swansea, Singleton Park

Where Daniel Jones was a student. Thomas, oddly, coupled it with London: two 'very big and bewildering places'. [CL, 90: to Trevor Hughes (early January 1934)].
Map 2 (p. 76).

## Uplands

In Thomas's day a middle-class residential suburb west of the town-centre, of which Cwmdonkin is the northern part.

*Letters:*
(i)   'a lowland collection of crossroads and shops'.
      [CL, 84: to Pamela Hansford Johnson (prob. early January 1934)].
(ii)  'A square, a handful of shops, a pub'.
      [CL, 146: to Pamela Hansford Johnson (c. 3 July 1934)].
(iii) For which he had been homesick, Thomas writes from Ireland.
      [CL, 191: to Bert Trick (prob. July 1935)]
(iv)  When he next visits Swansea, Thomas writes from Hampshire, he will be recognized by his 'belly, black hat, and a nostalgic flavour of the Uplands'.
      [CL, 364: to Bert Trick (March 1939)].

*Uplands and Uplands Hotel*

*Works:*

(i) Where Thomas and Raymond Price begin their hike to Rhossilli. ['Who Do You Wish Was With Us?', *Portrait*, *CS*, 196].

(ii) Patricia and the weeping Edith embarrass the small boy: he may be seen by 'a sneering, bigger boy from the Uplands'. ['Patricia, Edith, and Arnold', *Portrait*, *CS*, 148].

(iii) Thomas lived, says the Narrator, 'up the Uplands'. To the Uplands he goes in search of Thomas as a boy. ['Return Journey', *CS*, 318, 326-8].

Map 4 (p. 78).

*Uplands Cinema, Glanmor Road*
'the flea pit' was demolished to make way for Lloyds Bank. Thomas and his boyhood friends were regulars.

(i) First Voice recalls the boy as a noisy 'participant' in cowboy films. ['Return Journey', *CS*, 327].

(ii) Leslie and the narrator examine the 'stills' and reminisce about cinema-going. ['The Followers', *CS*, 332].

Map 4 (p. 78).

*Uplands Crescent*

(i) Through which Thomas and Raymond Price walk on their hike to Rhossilli. ['Who Do You Wish Was With Us?', *Portrait*, *CS*, 196].

(ii) Where Ron Bishop used to live. ['A Fine Beginning', *ST*, *CS*, 249, 255].

Map 4 (p. 78).

*Uplands Hotel in late 1970s*

## Uplands Hotel

The 'Uplands pub' where Thomas was the most regular of 'regulars'. The pub still exists but is now a 'theme-pub' called 'The Streets', in which 'Dylan Thomas' is one of the themes. The atmosphere has gone but the pub is worth visiting — once — as an example of cultural vandalism that would have taxed even Thomas's capacity for satire.

A visit to the 'Uplands Hotel' is part of his 'Provincial Rhythm'.

[CL, 84: to Pamela Hansford Johnson (prob. early January 1934)].

Map 4 (p. 78).

## Uplands Square

Through which Thomas and Raymond Price pass as they hike to Rhossilli.

['Who Do You Wish Was With Us?', Portrait, CS, 196].

Map 4 (p. 78).

## Upper Killay

The suburb that ends at Fairwood Common, where the Gower Peninsula begins. Thomas and Raymond Price pass through *en route* for Rhossilli.

['Who Do You Wish Was With Us?', Portrait, CS, 197].

## Vetch Field

See *Swansea Town A.F.C.*, above.

*Victoria Corner*

**Victoria Corner**
Once the main entrance to Victoria Park.
Its site is now occupied by the main
entrance to the Guildhall.
   Where Leslie and the narrator part.
['The Followers', *CS*, 336].
Map 4 (p. 78).

**Victoria Gardens**
See *Victoria Park*, below.

**Victoria Park**
As 'Victoria Gardens' it is where the
young man first sees Lou: ' "I saw a girl in
Victoria Gardens . . . She was a bit of God
help us all right",' he tells the barman.
['One Warm Saturday', *Portrait*, *CS*, 223.

See also, 221-2, 225-6, 228-9, 233].
Map 4 (p. 78).

**Victoria Saloon**
See *Bay View Hotel*, above.

**Vivian's Stream**
This runs to the sea parallel to the Brynmill wall of Singleton Park. In Thomas's
day it flowed under Mumbles Road and on
to the beach at the Brynmill Arch.
   Young Thomas used to play in the
water, says the Promenade-Man.
['Return Journey', *CS*, 325].
Map 4 (p. 78).

*Victoria Park in 1932*

*Walter Road and Walter Road Congregational Church*

*Walter Road*

*Letters:*
(i) 'a long, treed road'.
   [*CL*, 146: to Pamela Hansford Johnson (c. 3 July 1934)].
(ii) Is Fred Janes 'expressing down
   Walters road with his head full of
   fruit and stars?' enquires Thomas,
   from Hampshire, about his close
   friend, the painter Alfred Janes.
   [*CL*, 364: to Bert Trick (March
   1939)].

*Works:*
(i) Up which Thomas and Dan Jenkyn
   swagger home after their fight.
   ['The Fight', *Portrait*, *CS*, 154].
(ii) As 'Stanley Road' it is, for Samuel
   Bennet, where the Girls' School
   stands.

['A Fine Beginning', *ST*, *CS*, 241].
(iii) Where Thomas the young journalist
   covered a Sunday School outing.
   ['Return Journey', *CS*, 321].
Map 4 (p. 78).

*Walter Road Congregational Church*
Demolished to make way for a block of
flats. Thomas was sent there as a very
young child.
Map 3 (p. 77).

*Watkin Street, Mount Pleasant*
Seen by the Narrator as he stands in
bombed High Street.
['Return Journey', *CS*, 316].
Map 3 (p. 77).

*Wind Street, with Metropole Hotel, in 1937*

*Wind Street*
I wish, Thomas writes nostalgically from
Laugharne, to have 'smuts in my eye in
Wind Street'.
[*CL*, 434: to Charles Fisher (December
1939)].
Map 3 (p. 77).


*Woolworth's, 239 High Street*
Closed.
*Letter:*
The waitresses were often taken out.
[*CL*, 182: to Charles Fisher (early 1935)].
*Works:*
(i)   Where Lou had bought her white
      rose.
      ['One Warm Saturday', *Portrait, CS,*
      222].
(ii)  Out of which Mrs Constable charges.

['Old Garbo', *Portrait, CS,* 208].
Map 3 (p. 77).


*Workhouse, Mount Pleasant*
Now Mount Pleasant Hospital.
Thomas includes the 'Workhouse' in his
list of the district's main features.
[*CL*, 146: to Pamela Hansford Johnson
(c. 3 July 1934)].
Map 3 (p. 77).

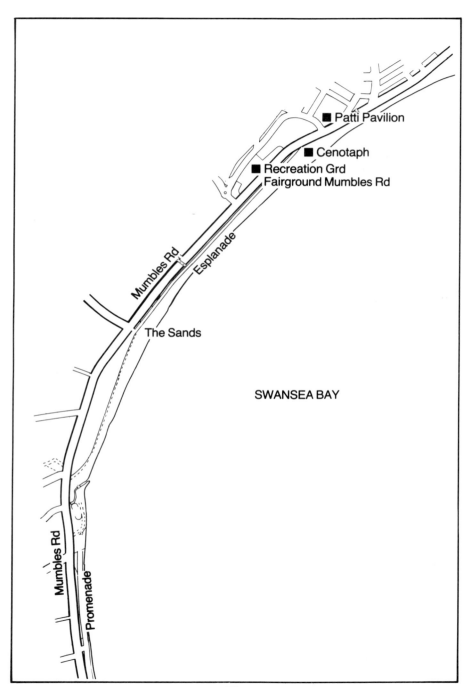

Patti Pavilion

Cenotaph

Recreation Grd
Fairground Mumbles Rd

Mumbles Rd

Esplanade

The Sands

SWANSEA BAY

Mumbles Rd

Promenade

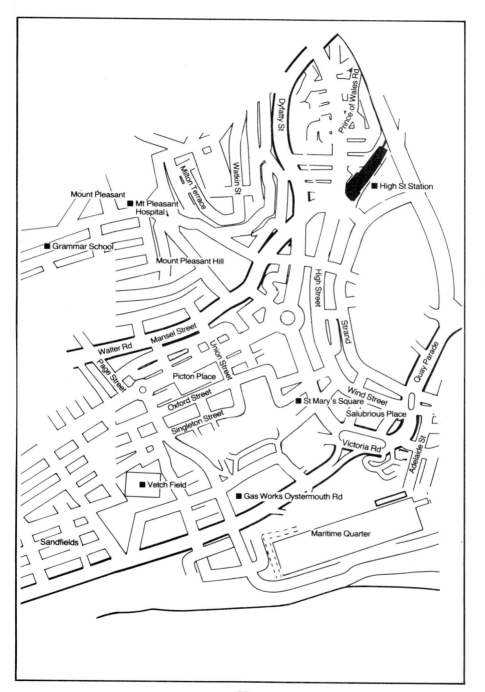

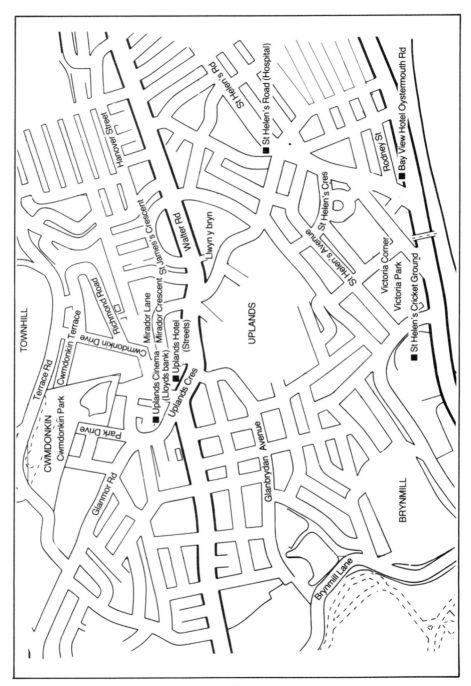

TOWNHILL

CWMDONKIN

Cwmdonkin Park

Terrace Rd

Park Drive

Glanmor Rd

Cwmdonkin Terrace

Cwmdonkin Drive

Richmond Road

Hanover Street

Mirador Lane

Mirador Crescent

St James's Crescent

Walter Rd

Llwyn y bryn

St Helen's Rd

St Helen's Road (Hospital)

Rodney St

Bay View Hotel Oystermouth Rd

St Helen's Cres

St Helen's Avenue

Victoria Corner

Victoria Park

St Helen's Cricket Ground

Uplands Cinema (Lloyds bank)

Uplands Hotel (Streets)

Uplands Cres

UPLANDS

Glanbrydan Avenue

BRYNMILL

Brynmill Lane

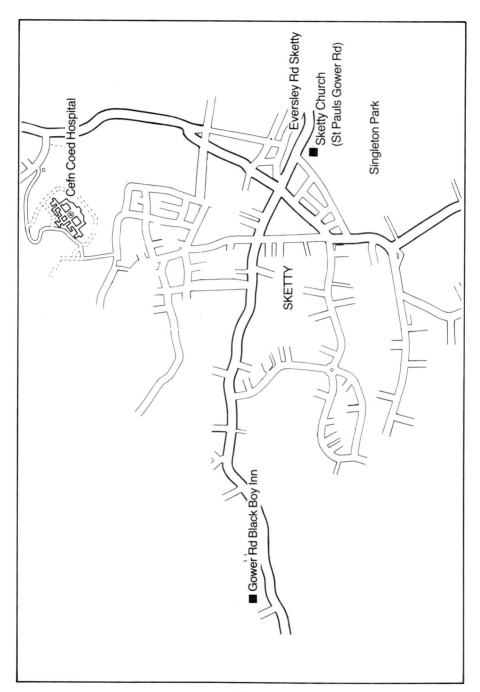

Cefn Coed Hospital

Eversley Rd Sketty

Sketty Church
(St Pauls Gower Rd)

Singleton Park

SKETTY

Gower Rd Black Boy Inn

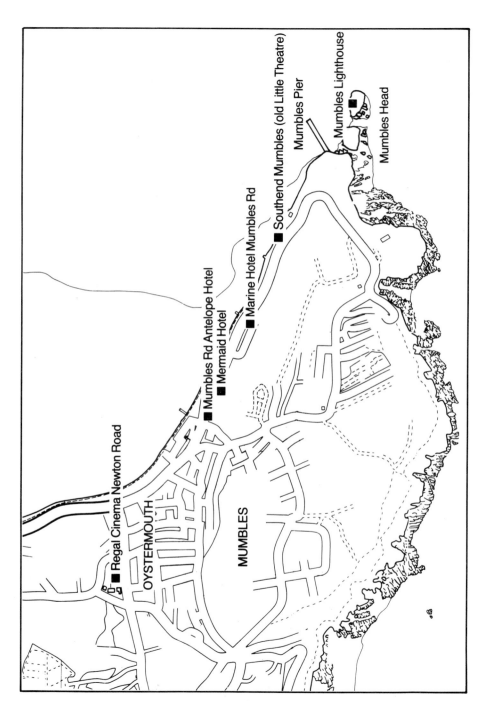

Regal Cinema Newton Road

OYSTERMOUTH

MUMBLES

Mumbles Rd Antelope Hotel

Mermaid Hotel

Marine Hotel Mumbles Rd

Southend Mumbles (old Little Theatre)

Mumbles Pier

Mumbles Lighthouse

Mumbles Head

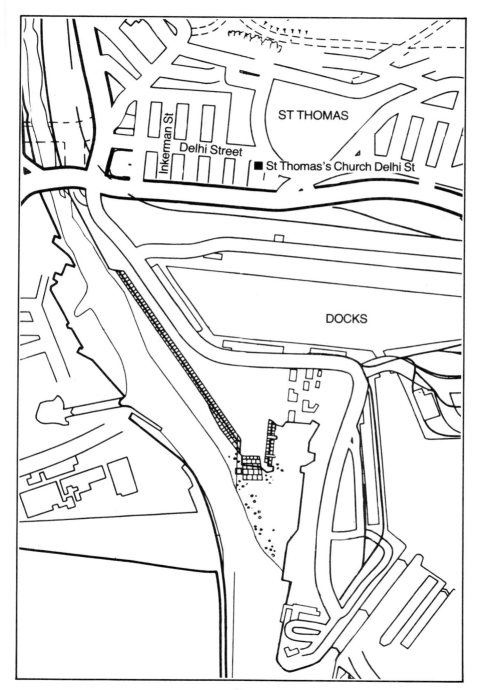

ST THOMAS

Inkerman St

Delhi Street

■ St Thomas's Church Delhi St

DOCKS

CHAPTER TWO

# GOWER

# 'communing with
...the quietness'

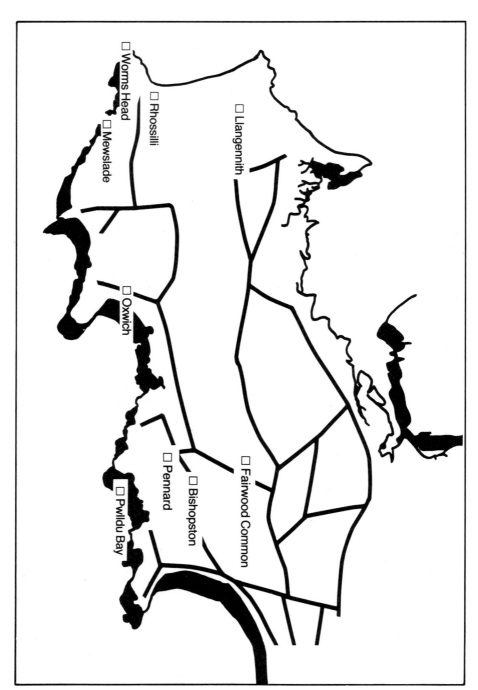

☐ Worms Head

☐ Rhossilli

☐ Mewslade

☐ Llangennith

☐ Oxwich

☐ Pennard

☐ Bishopston

☐ Fairwood Common

☐ Pwlldu Bay

84

The Gower peninsula, rich in natural beauty and magnificent coastal scenery, is 19 miles long and within easy reach of Swansea. For Thomas it was a crucial place. During schoolboy summers he camped there with his friends, often for weeks at a time; when a young man he often walked the coast-line alone, or with friends, stopping at convenient pubs. As he told Pamela Hansford Johnson, whom he took there when she visited Swansea, he was attracted by the area's beauty and, then, its quietness. It was also, so he said, the scene of amorous adventures vividly described by Paul Ferris in Chapter Five of *Dylan Thomas*, the standard biography.

Thomas's youthful memories of Gower provide material for his *Portrait* stories: 'Extraordinary Little Cough' and 'Who Do You Wish Was With Us?'. And the scenery, in particular the seascapes, cliffs, and wild-life, was an important general influence on his poetry.

REFERENCES TO GOWER

## Letters

(i)    Thomas, eager to impress the girl whom he had not then met, describes after-noons 'walking alone over the very desolate Gower cliffs, communing with the cold and the quietness'.
[*CL*, 85: to Pamela Hansford Johnson (prob. early January 1934)].

(ii)   'one of the loveliest sea-coast stretches in the whole of Britain'.
[*CL*, 62: to Pamela Hansford Johnson (early December 1933)].

(iii)  From Marshfield, near Chippenham (see Chapter Six), where the Thomases were staying with John Davenport, Dylan reveals to Vernon Watkins his horror of World War Two. In particular, he writes, 'I can't imagine Gower bombed'.
[*CL*, 463 (Summer 1940)].

## Works

(i)    Where young Thomas went to camp with George Hooping, Sidney Evans and Dan Davies.
['Extraordinary Little Cough', *Portrait, CS*, 165].

(ii)   'the ash-white of the road, the common heathers, the green and blue of fields and fragmentary sea'.
['Who Do You Wish Was With Us?', *Portrait, CS*, 198. See also, 196, 201].

*Bishopston*

*Bishopston*

A Gower village near Swansea to which Thomas's parents moved from Cwm-donkin in April 1937, following his father's retirement from teaching. His parents lived at 'Marston', Bishopston, until Spring 1941.

Dylan and family stayed at 'Marston' during 1940, January / February 1941 and again during early April 1941.

(i)   'a crowded piece of beautiful land-scape'.
      [*CL*, 390: to Henry Treece (July 1939)].

(ii)  'God's least favourite place'.
      [*CL*, 485 (22 May 1941)].

Map 8 (p. 83).

*Fairwood Common*

'the spreading heathered common . . . in the heat mist wasting for miles on either side'.
['Who Do You Wish Was With Us?', *Portrait*, *CS*, 197-8].
Map 8 (p. 83).

*Llangennith*

'very near nowhere'.
[*CL*, 114: to Pamela Hansford Johnson (15 April 1934)].
Map 8 (p. 83).

*Mewslade*

Where the campers bathe.
['Extraordinary Little Cough', *Portrait*, *CS*, 169].
Map 8 (p. 83).

*Fairwood Common at Upper Killay*

*'The Garth', Pennard*

## Oxwich

'Down there is Oxwich, but you can't see it', says Ray Price to young Thomas as they walk the main road to Rhossilli. ['Who Do You Wish Was With Us?', *Portrait*, *CS*, 198. See also, 199]. Map 8 (p. 83).


## Pennard

Thomas's close friend, Vernon Watkins, the distinguished poet, lived with his family overlooking the sea at 'The Garth', Heatherslade, Pennard Cliffs. Thomas, Caitlin, and friends, visited often and sometimes played croquet on the lawn. Map 8 (p. 83).

## Pwlldu Bay

(i) One of the names Thomas says he has difficulty pronouncing.
[*CL*, 24: to Pamela Hansford Johnson (15 October 1933)].

(ii) 'comfortable, wild Pwll Du'.
[*CL*, 460 (prob. 8 August 1940)].

### Pwlldu Inn

Mis-spelled (partly phonetically) by Thomas as 'Pwlldee'. He is referring to what was, in his day, the 'Beaufort Arms'. It is now the first of two houses close to the beach. When having lunch outside the old 'Beaufort' Thomas reports seeing a rat.
[*CL*, 95-6: to Pamela Hansford Johnson (prob. 1934)].

Map 8 (p. 83).

*Pwlldu & Beaufort*

*Rhossilli Bay*

## Rhossilli

The furthermost point of the peninsula. Rhossilli has a five-miles-long arc of beautiful beach with spectacular cliffs. The young Thomas spent summers here camping with his friends, probably at nearby Pilton Green. Before moving to the Boat House Thomas considered living at The Old Rectory near the beach. But — then — Rhossilli had no pub.

*Letters:*

(i) 'The bay is the wildest, bleakest, and barrennest I know'.
[*CL*, 62: to Pamela Hansford Johnson (prob. early December 1933)].

(ii) 'I wish I were in Rhossilli', he writes from Oxfordshire.
[*CL*, 693 (23 November 1948)].

*Works:*

(i) (a) Much of the story is set at or near Rhossilli where young Thomas camps with school-friends.
(b) George Hooping runs the whole length of the beach because the school bullies, Brazell and Skully, said they had done so.
['Extraordinary Little Cough', *Portrait*, *CS*, 173. See also, 165, 166, 168, 170, 172].

(ii) (a) Ray Price and young Thomas head for Rhossilli.
(b) They gaze from the cliffs at the 'very long golden beach'.
['Who Do You Wish Was With Us?', *Portrait*, *CS*, 199, 200].
Map 8 (p. 83).

*Worm's Head*

## Worm's Head

A one-mile-long promontory at the southern end of Rhossilli Bay, accessible only at low tide.

*Letter:*
'the very promontory of depression'.
[*CL*, 62: to Pamela Hansford Johnson (prob. early December 1933)].

*Work:*
Where Ray Price and young Thomas are cut off by the tide: 'the humped and serpentine body . . . the great rock poised between sky and sea . . . "It's too wild for a townee", I said'.
['Who Do You Wish Was With Us?',

*Portrait*, *CS*, 200–1. See also, 196, 199, 203, 305].
Map 8 (p. 83).

# CHAPTER THREE

# LAUGHARNE

## 'this wet idyllic tomb'

Laugharne is on the western shore of the Taf estuary in what is now south Dyfed but what was — and still is for sensible folk — the southern part of Carmarthenshire. To the east, on the squat peninsula between the estuaries of the Taf and the Towy, are Llangain, Llanstephan, Llanybri, and Fernhill, the area where Thomas so often stayed as a child with his mother's relations (see Chapter Four). For crows that fly straight Laugharne is barely three miles west of Llanybri, but, in ethos and atmosphere, it is worlds away. In a fiercely Welsh-speaking area, Laugharne, with its Portreeve and Georgian buildings, is an English-speaking enclave, a beautiful, isolated, eccentric, quiet place just right for an unconventional Swansea man with little Welsh and rural leanings.

'Laugharne imagery' (the estuary, herons, sea-birds, local scenery) permeates Thomas's work. *Under Milk Wood* celebrates the spirit of the place. The following works, either wholly or in part, have recognizable 'Laugharne' settings:

(a) *Poems*

'To take to give is all, return what given' (*Notebooks* version only)
'When I woke'
'Poem in October'
'Over Sir John's Hill'
'Poem on his Birthday'
'Prologue'

(b) *Prose*

'Laugharne'
*Under Milk Wood*

REFERENCES TO LAUGHARNE

*Letters*

(i)   Thomas writes during his first recorded visit to Laugharne. The weather is cold and windy, the place quiet; he is fascinated by 'the strangest town in Wales . . . Today . . . a hell-mouthed mist is blowing over the Laugharne ferry'.
[*CL*, 136: to Pamela Hansford Johnson (11 May 1934)].

(ii) Still urging his girl-friend to visit Swansea, Thomas promises her a look at Laugharne, 'the nearest approach under the sun to a Stygian borough'.
[*CL*, 146: to Pamela Hansford Johnson (c. 3 July 1934)].

(iii) Thomas writes from his home in Gosport Street to Henry Treece, the poet, novelist and critic, looking forward to welcoming him to a town that has 'three good pubs . . . the best bottled mild in England'.
[*CL*, 304: to Henry Treece (16 June 1938)].

(iv) The Thomases, deeply in debt, plan to remove themselves, temporarily, from 'Seaview'. Laugharne is 'a lovely town', but full of creditors.
[*CL*, 332: to Henry Treece (mid-October 1938)].

(v) Thomas describes the horror and terror induced in him by 'this war, trembling even on the edge of Laugharne . . . Laugharne is a little Danzig' ('Danzig' is the Polish port now known as Gdansk, a flash-point during World War Two).
[*CL*, 401: (c. 25 August 1939)].

(vi) During the early days of the War Laugharne is a refuge but a rather quiet one. He hopes that his old Swansea friend will visit 'this cockled city . . . sweet and quiet . . . so slow and prettily sad'.
[*CL*, 416-7: to Bert Trick (29 September 1939)].

(vii) Thomas, still in 'Seaview', is homesick for Swansea and looks forward to a Christmas reunion there. Meanwhile, in Laugharne, 'the castle and the pretty water make me sick'.
[*CL*, 434: to Charles Fisher (December 1939)].

(viii) From South Leigh, Oxfordshire, Thomas wrote to his generous benefactor, then the wife of A. J. P. Taylor, about the possibility of renting the house in Laugharne once occupied by the famous novelist Richard Hughes: 'the best town, the best house, the only castle, the mapped, measured, inhabited, drained, garaged, townhalled, pubbed and churched, shopped, gulled, and estuaried one state of happiness!'
[*CL*, 689-90: to Margaret Taylor (prob. October 1948)].

(ix) 'Princess Caetani' was a rich American living in Rome. She subsidized *Botteghe Oscure*, the international literary magazine that published much of Thomas's later work, including 'Over Sir John's Hill', 'Do not go gentle', and part of *Under Milk Wood*. Writing from the Boat House he apologises at length for not sending more of the play (he hadn't finished it and had been, again, to America) and describes graphically how circumstances (mainly financial) press upon him. Even the 'weather gets me like poverty: it blurs and then blinds, creeps chalky and crippling into the bones, shrouds me in wet self, rains away the world'.

[*CL*, 844: to Marguerite Caetani (6 November 1952)].
(x)   Charles Fry was head of Allen Wingate the publishers; Thomas had failed to
deliver a commissioned book on America. His letter shows him desperately
concerned about his work: he is writing very little and with increasing difficulty. In more ways than one Laugharne seems to have become 'this wet
idyllic tomb on the coast'.
[*CL*, 869: to Charles Fry (16 February 1953)].
(xi)  For Brinnin, see Chapter Seven. Fresh from his third American visit
Laugharne, to Thomas, means 'torpor and rain and Ivy's dungeon' (i.e.
Brown's Hotel, kept by Ivy Williams).
[*CL*, 893: to John Malcolm Brinnin (16 June 1953)].

## *Works*

(i)   Thomas grieves at having done no work
'In summer Laugharne among the cockle boats
And by the castle with the boatlike birds'.
['To take to give is all, return what given', *Notebooks*, 303. The lines are not in
the final version: 'On no work of words', *PDJ*, 140].
(ii)  'my sea town'.
['When I woke', *PDJ*, 150].
(iii) 'this timeless, beautiful, barmy (both spellings) town . . . a legendary lazy
little black-magical bedlam by the sea'.
['Laugharne', *QEOM*, 70-2].

*Boathouse*

## Boat House

Apart from a period at Delancey Street, Camden Town, London, and visits to the U.S.A., this was home for the Thomases from April/May 1949 until Dylan's death on 9 November 1953. Whilst they lived here the Thomases' youngest child was born on 24 July 1949. Hence his name: Colm Garan, 'Garan' being Welsh for 'heron'.

*Letters:*

(i) 'this is *it*: the place, the house, the workroom, the time'.
   [*CL*, 706: to Margaret Taylor (c. 11 May 1949)].

(ii) 'this tumbling house whose every broken pane and wind-whipped-off slate, childscrawled wall, rain-stain, mousehole, knobble and ricket, man-booby-and-rat-trap, I know in my sleep'.
   [*CL*, 844: to Madame Caetani (6 November 1952)].

*Work:*

'my seashaken house
On a breakneck of rocks'.
['Prologue', *PDJ*, 3].

## Brown's Hotel, King Street

Thomas's favourite Laugharne pub. A walk to 'moulder in Brown's' was part of his daily routine.
[*CL*, 910: to Daniel Jones (24 August 1953)].

## Castle

During the 1930s and 40s this was rented by the distinguished novelist Richard Hughes, who lived in a house in the castle

*Brown's Hotel*

*Castle*

grounds (see *'The Castle'*, below). In Hughes's gazebo on the castle walls, in 1938, Thomas wrote part of *Portrait of the Artist as a Young Dog.*

(i)  'the castle
     Brown as owls.
     ['Poem in October', *PDJ*, 177].

(ii) 'the collapsed castle'.
     ['The Crumbs of One Man's Year', *CS*, 314].

## 'The Castle'

The Georgian house adjoining the castle in which Richard Hughes lived. The Thomases stayed with him from April/May 1941 to August 1941.

## Corporation Arms, Gosport Street

A pub sometimes used by Thomas.

*Gazebo on Castle Walls*

*Estuary*

*2 Gosport Street*

*Cross House Inn, The Grist*
A pub much used by Thomas.

*Estuary*
Of the river Taf.
(i) 'the estuary pool . . . where . . . children rolled together in original mud'.
['The Crumbs of One Man's Year', *CS*, 314].
(ii) 'my dabbed bay'.
['Prologue', *PDJ*, 4].

*2 Gosport Street*
From May 1938 to July 1938 Dylan and Caitlin lived here in a cottage named 'Eros': 'pokey and ugly, four rooms like stained boxes'.
[*CL*, 304: to Henry Treece (16 June 1938)].

*The Grist*
This small square in the lower part of Laugharne is the site of the 'stunted' War Memorial.
[*CL*, 402: to D. J. Thomas (29 August 1939)].

*Harbour*
(i) 'the dwindling harbour'.
['Poem in October', *PDJ*, 177].
(ii) 'Crystal harbour vale
Where the sea cobbles sail'.
['Over Sir John's Hill', *PDJ*, 202].

*Manchester House, King Street*
According to Ackerman (*Welsh Dylan*, 121) this suggested Mr Mog Edwards's draper's emporium.
[*UMW*, 37, 49].

*Sea View*

See also, Chapter Four, *New Quay / Manchester House.*


## 49 Orchard Park Estate

Dolly Long lived here, with whom the Thomases left two-years-old Colm when they went to the U.S.A. in 1952.


## *The Pelican, King Street*

The house opposite Brown's Hotel where Thomas's parents lived from May 1949. Thomas's body lay here before his funeral

*Pelican*

## *St Martin's Church*

Thomas's funeral took place here on 24 November 1953. He is buried in the adjoining graveyard, the grave marked by a plain wooden cross inscribed:

In
Memory
of
DYLAN THOMAS
Died
Nov. 9
1953

R.I.P.

'the sea wet church the size of a snail'. ['Poem in October', *PDJ*, 177].

*Grave*

*Sea View*
A four-storied house near the castle. The Thomases lived here from July 1938 to July 1940.

*Sir John's Hill*
The hill to the south of Laugharne visible from the Boat House.
  'Sir John's elmed
Hill'.
['Over Sir John's Hill', *PDJ*, 202].

*Town Hall*
Its clock 'tells the time backwards'.
[*CL*, 689: to Margaret Taylor (prob. October 1948)].

*Wood*
Probably that on Sir John's Hill.
Thomas — in the Boat House — was at 'a wood's dancing hoof'.
['Prologue', *PDJ*, 3].

*St John's Hill*

*Town Hall*

*Work-Hut, Dylan's Walk*
Thomas's shack or shed on the cliff-path
behind the Boat House, which he used as a
study.
*Letter:*
'my wordsplashed hut'.
[*CL*, 844: to Madame Caetani (6 November 1952)].
*Work:*
'the long tongued room
. . . his slant, racking house'.
['Poem on his Birthday', *PDJ*, 209].

*Work-Hut*

101

CHAPTER FOUR

'the hymnal blob'

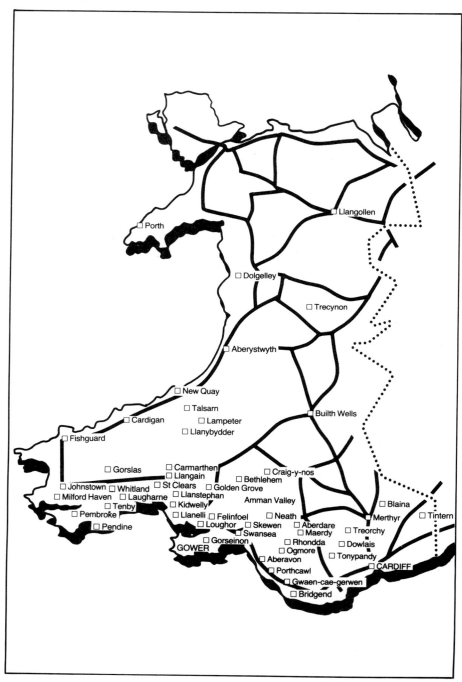

'One: I am a Welshman', Thomas once began an account of himself. But though he was born and bred in Wales and lived in Laugharne and New Quay for a substantial part of his adult life, his highly ambivalent response to his country is found mainly in scattered references. Apart from 'Wales and the Artist' in *Quite Early One Morning*, 'After the Funeral' [*PDJ*, 136-7], and the second half of 'Prologue' [*PDJ*, 4-5], he did not write at length about Wales as a country. He wrote much, of course, about particular Welsh places and, necessarily, all his work has a Welsh element. His whole personal and artistic stance was governed by the fact that he grew up and became a poet far away from metropolitan culture and outside England. That is, he never felt part of the 'respectable' literary establishment and, in his life as well as in his work, reacted against such important contemporary literary cliques as the 'Bloomsbury group', with its prissy, upper-middle-class aestheticism (see Chapter Five / *Bloomsbury*), and the social and intellectual poetry of W. H. Auden and his followers. Having said that, there is little doubt that Thomas considered Wales to be a cultural desert dominated by narrow-minded religion. His attacks on his homeland are partly because he was ashamed of what he regarded as his provincial origins and partly because he thought enough of his country to want it to be different. Thomas the Welshman is a tense, tangled and complex person.

REFERENCES TO WALES

*Letters*

(i)     Whilst still 'courting by correspondence' Thomas describes a bus journey through Carmarthenshire to Llangain. Each small town was 'a festering sore on the body of a dead country . . . I'm sick, and this bloody country's killing me'.
        [*CL*, 30: to Pamela Hansford Johnson (late October 1933)].

(ii)    To his former Swansea friend now living in Harrow he writes, slightly satirically, of 'the emptiness of Wales'.
        [*CL*, 89: to Trevor Hughes (early January 1934)].

(iii)   Stephen Spender, already well-known as a poet, wrote to Thomas to congratulate him on his poem 'Light breaks where no sun shines', following its publication in *The Listener*. Thomas's 'thank-you' note drifts easily into attacks on Swansea's provinciality and an insistence on 'my natural hatred of Wales'.

[*CL*, 100: to Stephen Spender (March 1934)].

(iv)   Having met Miss Johnson and stayed at her London home (see Chapter Five / *53 Battersea Rise*), Thomas urges her to visit him in Swansea: 'I, to you, move in a fabulous, Celtic land, surrounded by castles, tall black hats, the ghosts of accents, and eternal Eisteddfodau'.
[*CL*, 145: to Pamela Hansford Johnson (c. 3 July 1934)].

(v)   Thomas and friends had wrecked the meeting of a Swansea literary society with scandalous speeches, his own conduct revealing his desperate dissatisfaction with the life he then led. Wales is, he wrote, 'a land entirely peopled by perverts', and among the latter he included himself.
[*CL*, 172: to Pamela Hansford Johnson (October 1934)].

(vi)   Earp, a poet and a critic, was a London friend. Thomas writes from New Quay in Dyfed:
'where I sit in my combs
As safe and snug as a bugger in Rugby'.
[*CL,* 520: to T. W. Earp (1 September 1944)].

(vii)   For Tennant, see Chapter Five / *Gargoyle Club*. Desperate to find accommodation in London for himself and family, Thomas writes, to enlist Tennant's help, from 'mean, green, horse-thieving Wales'.
[*CL*, 564: to David Tennant (28 August 1945)].

(viii) John Nims was an American poet; he and his wife had been hospitable during Thomas's first American visit. He promises to return their kindness should they ever visit 'this arsehole of the universe, this hymnal blob, this pretty, sick, fond, sad Wales'.
[*CL*, 767: to Mr & Mrs John Nims (17 July 1950)].


## *Works*

(i)   The child's curtains are blown by Welsh winds.
['The Tree', *CS*, 6].

(ii)   (a) The base of Wales was once shaken by the fall of a mountain.
(b) Blackened, stunted trees are the remains of those crippled by a Welsh death.
['The Orchards', *CS*, 42, 45].

(iii)   'the loud hill of Wales' can be a source of profound, wordless communication.
['Especially when the October wind', *PDJ*, 99].

(iv) (a) Tom Twp meets a shadow who suggests measuring the Welsh undead.
(b) Mr Montgomery walks into Wales from his house of death.
['The Horse's Ha', *CS*, 60, 62].

(v) The wind blows from Wales on a lazy dying afternoon.
['A Prospect of the Sea', *CS*, 90].

(vi) (a) Where the Holy Six live.
(b) The trees in Jarvis valley are filled with Welsh birds.
['The Holy Six', *CS*, 95, 98, 99].

(vii) Ann Jones, when alive, was a fountain watering 'the parched worlds of Wales'.
['After the Funeral', *PDJ*, 136].

(viii) (a) Young Thomas imagines himself fighting a demon all over Wales for the sake of a girl from Swansea convent.
(b) He tells Gwilym that Mrs Williams is 'the richest woman in Wales'.
['The Peaches', *Portrait, CS*, 123, 129].

(ix) His fight with Dan Jenkyn gives young Thomas 'the best black eye in Wales'.
['The Fight', *Portrait, CS*, 154].

(x) Ray Price and young Thomas are 'wanderers in wild Wales'.
['Who Do You Wish Was With Us?', *Portrait, CS*, 197].

(xi) Through 'the lubber crust of Wales' the poet once burst like a rocket.
['Once below a time', *PDJ*, 151].

(xii) Outside Swansea, Thomas recalls, was 'a strange Wales, coal-pitted, mountained, river run, full . . . of choirs and football teams and sheep and story-book tall black hats and red flannel petticoats'.
['Reminiscences of Childhood (Second Version)', *QEOM*, 8; see also 9, 14].

(xiii) (a) Where the morning began quite early.
(b) The country to which the English male nurse had retired.
(c) At the far end of which was the town described in the story.
['Quite Early One Morning', *CS*, 291, 293, 295].

(xiv) (a) For the young boy a house on fire was better than all the cats of Wales standing in a row.
(b) Thomas's boyhood was long ago when Wales had wolves.
['A Child's Christmas in Wales', *CS*, 296-7, 297].

(xv) (a) Thomas, says the Narrator, was above average height for Wales: he was 'five foot six and a half'.
(b) The children of Mirador School chant the counties of Wales.
['Return Journey', *CS*, 318, 327].

(xvi) In the South Sea, says the Missionary feelingly, the rain is even worse than in Wales.

[*The Beach of Falesá*, 81].

(xvii) Wales is where it always seems to be raining.
[*Rebecca's Daughters*, 11].

(xviii) The dangers of anglicization *and* the dangers of Welsh parochialism are the subjects of this broadcast.
['Wales and the Artist', *QEOM*, 153-4].

(xix) (a) 'To Wales in my arms' begins the second half of the 'Prologue'.
(b) Thomas imagines riding out alone 'Under the stars of Wales'.
['Prologue', *PDJ*, 4, 5].

(xx) (a) A country over which alp-horns might blow.
(b) From which come lovers of music-making.
(c) In which other countries' representatives have gathered for
['The International Eisteddfod', *QEOM*, 59, 60, 62].

(xxi) The outing ends 'at the end of the world', meaning West Wales.
['A Story', *CS*, 343].

(xxii) (a) The 'Star of Wales' is one of the moored boats.
(b) For the Reverend Eli Jenkins Wales is 'Dear Gwalia!'
(c) 'Praise the Lord! We are a musical nation', is the Reverend's response to Pollie Garter's song.
(d) Dead Rosie Probert reminds Captain Cat:
'Between Frisco and Wales
You were my bosun.'
[*UMW*, 4, 24, 54, 69].

*Aberavon, West Glam.*
(i) Young Thomas, drinking in the back bar of 'The Three Lamps', is glad his father is visiting an uncle in Aberavon.
['Old Garbo', *Portrait*, *CS*, 211].
(ii) For whom the stranger played rugby in 1898, or so he said.
['A Story', *CS*, 344].
Map 9 (p. 104).

*Aberdare, Mid Glam.*
(i) Where the Fortune-Teller lived.
['After the Fair', *CS*, 2].

(ii) 'I had it bitten in Aberdare once', says the temptress about her damaged shoulder.
['Jarley's', *CS*, 350].
Map 9 (p. 104).

*Aberystwyth, Dyfed*
The university town where Thomas's father, D. J. Thomas, was a student. He graduated from University College of Wales, Aberystwyth, in 1899, with first-class honours in English.

During October 1934 Thomas spent a week-end in the town with the short-story writer and novelist Caradoc Evans.

(i) Mr Stul, 'the horny man', is 'the father of Aberystwyth's bastards'. ['The Holy Six', *CS*, 100].

(ii) Where Mr Griffiths got his degree. ['Quite Early One Morning', *CS*, 294].

(iii) Birthplace of Sir Henry's cat. [*Rebecca's Daughters*, 13].

(iv) Where Hetty went on a choir-outing with her sister Katinka. ['The Followers', *CS*, 336].

Map 9 (p. 104).

*Aled, Gwynedd*
One of the rivers listed in the Rev. Eli Jenkins's verses in praise of Llaregyb. [*UMW*, 25].

*Amman Valley, Dyfed*
Where the boy comes from. ['A Prospect of the Sea', *CS*, 90]. Map 9 (p. 104).

*Berwyn Hills, Clwyd*
To the south-west of Llangollen. ['The International Eisteddfod', *QEOM*, 58].

*Bethlehem, Dyfed*
Where there is 'a prison for mad women'. ['The School for Witches', *CS*, 65]. Map 9 (p. 104).

*Blaen Cwm, Dyfed*
See *Llangain*, below.

*Blaina, Gwent*
Home of the collier who rang the fair's

strength-machine.
['Holiday Memory', *CS*, 309].
Map 9 (p. 104).

*Bridgend, Mid Glam.*
(i) A town 'roaring with temptation', visited by Gwilym during a religious tour on which he met — he said — many actresses. ['The Peaches', *Portrait*, *CS*, 128].

(ii) In Bridgend, says Tom, the birds are affected by the munition works: 'You can always tell a cuckoo from Bridgend, it goes "Cuckbloodyoo! cuckbloodyoo!"'.
['Just Like Little Dogs', *Portrait*, *CS*, 177].
Map 9 (p. 104).

*Builth Wells, Powys*
A vegetarian ornithologist in Builth Wells wishes to become Mrs Ogmore-Pritchard's lodger. She has 'got a man in Builth Wells', says First Woman, maliciously.
[*UMW*, 39, 40, 45].
Map 9 (p. 104).

*Cader Idris, Gwynedd*
(i) In Thomas's early stories are a number of references to a half-imaginary region vaguely located near Cader Idris mountain. 'Capel Cader', 'Cader House', 'Cader Marshes', 'Cader Peak' and 'Idris Water' are landmarks in a world of strange, surrealistic sexuality.
['The Orchards', *CS*, 48; 'The School for Witches', *CS*, 65-71; 'A Prospect of the Sea', *CS*, 88; 'The Map of Love', *CS*, 110, 112, 113].

(ii) '. . . tempest-torn', says the Rev. Eli Jenkins in his verses in praise of Llaregyb.
[*UMW*, 24].

## Cardiff, South Glam.

(i) What the girl is called and where she appears to come from.
['After the Fair', *CS*, 2, 3].
(ii) Where cries can be heard.
['The Horses's Ha', *CS*, 59].
(iii) Mr O'Brien is 'a broth of a man about Cardiff'.
['One Warm Saturday', *Portrait*, *CS*, 230].

### Tiger Bay
Cardiff's once-notorious dockland.
'A girl from Tiger Bay held Jarvis close'.
['The Map of Love', *CS*, 113].
Map 9 (p. 104).

## Cardigan, Dyfed
A 'filthy town', thought Thomas.
[*CL*, 531 (15 November 1944)].
Map 9 (p. 104).

## Cardigan Bay, Dyfed
'Sinister dark over Cardigan Bay'.
['New Quay', verse-letter to T. W. Earp, *PDJ*, 179].
Map 9 (p. 104).

## Cardiganshire, Dyfed
*Letter:*
When telephoning from a Cardiganshire pub Thomas was troubled by 'the buzzing of those Cardy drones'.
[*CL*, 271: to Donald Taylor (8 February 1945)].
*Works:*
(i) In Mr Evans' contribution to the friends' novel, *Where Tawe Flows*, Mary leaves her father to live with her uncle in Cardiganshire.
['Where Tawe Flows', *Portrait*, *CS*, 192].
(ii) Over which darkness came 'psalming'.
['A Pub Poem', *PDJ*, 242].

## Carew, Dyfed
The Carew tollgate features in this film-script of nineteenth-century rioting.
[*Rebecca's Daughters*, 129, 132].

## Carmarthen, Dyfed
The nearest sizable place to Laugharne.
(i) The boy imagines the girl inducing Carmarthen tigers to attack him.
['A Prospect of the Sea', *CS*, 89].
(ii) (a) The parson's ducks had been bought at Carmarthen fair.
(b) The search for Grandpa takes young Thomas and the Johnstown villagers to Carmarthen in a pony-trap.
['A Visit to Grandpa's, *Portrait*, *CS*, 140, 141].
(iii) Gwilym bought his keys in a junk-shop there.
['The Peaches', *Portrait*, *CS*, 128. See also, 132].
(iv) Mr Phillips gets drunk at Carmarthen mart.
['Where Tawe Flows', *Portrait*, *CS*, 190].
(v) 'Carmarthen' rhymes with 'penny-

farthen' in Augustus's song.
[*Me and My Bike*, 47].

(vi) (a) Where the jail is and where there are riots.

(b) 'There's a nice town', says Lewis the turnpike man.
[*Rebecca's Daughters*, 12, 27, 29].

(vii) Mog Edwards the draper has a delivery of ribbons from Carmarthen that he wishes to give to Miss Myfanwy Price.
[*UMW*, 49].

*Boar's Head Hotel, Lammas Street*
A pub much used by Thomas during his frequent visits from Laugharne.

*Constitution Hill*
Up which go young Thomas and the

*Boar's Head, Carmarthen*

Johnstown villagers as they search for Grandpa.
['A Visit to Grandpa's', *Portrait*, *CS*, 142].

*Infirmary*
Thomas's aunt, Ann Jones of Fernhill Farm, the subject of 'After the Funeral', died here in 1933. His second son, Colm Garan, was born here on 24 July 1949.

*Lammas Street*
Through which young Thomas and the Johnstown villagers search for Grandpa.
['A Visit to Grandpa's', *Portrait*, *CS*, 142].

*Towy Bridge*
Where young Thomas and the Johnstown villagers find Grandpa on his way to be buried in Llangadock.
['A Visit to Grandpa's', *Portrait*, *CS*, 142].
Map 9 (p. 104).

*Carmarthenshire, Dyfed*
The old county of Carmarthenshire — now part of Dyfed — was, for Thomas, an important and nostalgic place. His mother's family were Carmarthenshire people; his father was born in Johnstown; many relations still lived in the area. Thus, in 1949, when Thomas finally settled in Laugharne, on the county's southern coast, he was returning to his rural roots. See also, *Johnstown, Llangain, Llanybri*, below, and Chapter Three.

*Letters:*
(i) Thomas's mother came from the 'agricultural depths'.
[*CL*, 43: to Pamela Hansford Johnson

(early November 1933))].
(ii) Thomas hopes to spend every summer in the county.
[*CL*, 364: to Bert Trick (March
1939)].
(iii) 'the inbred crooked county'.
[*CL*, 558: to Oscar Williams (30 July
1945)].

*Works:*
(i) Lou is toasted in Swansea, by a
drunk ignorant of geography, as the
prettiest girl in Carmarthenshire.
['One Warm Saturday', *Portrait*, *CS*,
227].
(ii) 'We've left her under a table in Carmarthenshire', complains Mr Hum-
phries of Mr Evans's story about
Mary Phillips on her farm.
['Where Tawe Flows', *Portrait*, *CS*,
188, 191].

*Carnedd Llewellyn, Gwynedd*
'. . . beauty born', intones the Rev. Eli
Jenkins in his verses in praise of Llaregyb.
[*UMW*, 24].

*Cathmarw*
A joke: in English it means 'dead cat'.
(i) Cathmarw hamlet is the story's setting.
['The Horse's Ha', *CS*, 61, 62, 63].
(ii) (a) Where a black girl screamed in
labour.
(b) Where the metamorphosed dusts
danced.
['The School for Witches', *CS*, 65,
70].

*Cathmarw Hill*
The light breaks over it.

['The Lemon', *CS*, 58].
See *Cathmarw* above.

*Claerwen, Clwyd*
A river listed by the Rev. Eli Jenkins in his
verses in praise of Llaregyb.
[*UMW*, 25].

*Cleddau, Dyfed*
A river listed by the Rev. Eli Jenkins in his
verses in praise of Llaregyb.
[*UMW*, 25].

*Craigynos, Powys*
Where Ray Price's sister Brenda is in a
sanatorium.
['Who Do You Wish Was With Us?', *Por-
trait*, *CS*, 203].
Map 9 (p. 104).

*Daw, Dyfed*
An anglicized abbreviation of Dau-
gleddyf, a Pembrokeshire river listed in
the Rev. Eli Jenkins's verses in praise of
Llaregyb.
[*UMW*, 25].

*Dee, Clwyd*
(i) The river that runs through Llangollen.
['The International Eisteddfod',
*QEOM*, 58, 62].
(ii) Listed in the Rev. Eli Jenkins's verses
in praise of Llarebyg.
[*UMW*, 25].

*Dewi, Dyfed*
A tributary of the Taf. The Rev. Eli Jenkins describes it as flowing through Llaregyb.
[*UMW*, 17, 23, 25].


*Dinas Bran, Clwyd*
A castle near Llangollen.
Thomas wants a great alp-horn to blow amidst the ruins.
['The International Eisteddfod', *QEOM*, 59].
Map 9 (p. 104).


*Dolgelley, Gwynedd*
Jarvis lay 'with a virgin from Dolgelley'.
['The Map of Love', *CS*, 113].
Map 9 (p. 104).

*Dovey, Gwynedd*
A river listed in the Rev. Eli Jenkins's verses in praise of Llaregyb.
[*UMW*, 25].


*Dowlais, Mid Glam.*
*Letter:*
Fan-mail from Dowlais will be, Thomas considers, highly unlikely.
[*CL*, 377: to John Davenport (11 May 1939)].
*Works*
(i)  Where the drunk suffered an industrial accident:
  ' "When did he lose his bottom?" said Mrs Franklin.
  "When Gabriel blew his whistle down in Dowlais",' explains the barman.

*Dowlais* (Air Photo)

['One Warm Saturday', *Portrait*, *CS*, 225, 227].
(ii) ' "How's the tenors in Dowlais?", ' asks Third Drowned.
[*UMW*, 6].
Map 9 (p. 104).


*Dulais, Mid Glam.*
A river listed in the Rev. Eli Jenkins's verses in praise of Llaregyb.
[*UMW*, 25].


*Eden, Gwynedd*
A river listed in the Rev. Eli Jenkins's verses in praise of Llaregyb.
[*UMW*, 25].


*Edw, Powys*
A river listed in the Rev. Eli Jenkins's verses in praise of Llaregyb.
[*UMW*, 25].


*Edwinsford Arms, Dyfed*
See *Llangain*, below.


*Ely, Mid Glam.*
A river listed in the Rev. Eli Jenkins's verses in praise of Llaregyb.
[*UMW*, 25].


*Felinfoel, Dyfed*
Home of 'Felinfoel', the famous West Wales beer.

Thomas remembers himself as a young man 'whose water's Felinfoel, that nut-brown prince'.

[*CL*, 373: to Henry Treece (prob. May 1939)].
Map.


*Fernhill, Dyfed*
See *Llangain*, below.


*Fishguard, Dyfed*
As 'Fishinguard' this is the place to which William Evans's daughter eloped with a deaf barber.
[*Rebecca's Daughters*, 27].
Map 9 (p. 104).


*Glamorganshire*
(i) Where the sea and the shore meet violently.
['The Orchards', *CS*, 42].
(ii) (a) The poet asks 'time' to stop 'on Glamorgan's hill'.
(b) He celebrates 'Golden Glamorgan', its sky full of descending hawks.
['Hold Hard, these ancient minutes in the cuckoo's month', *PDJ*, 122, 123].
(iii) Jarvis's fingers hold 'Glamorgan's canker'.
['The Map of Love', *CS*, 113].
(iv) Lou corrects a drunk who thinks she is in Carmarthenshire.
['One Warm Saturday', *Portrait*, *CS*, 227].


*Golden Grove, Dyfed*
As a celebrated beauty-spot, 'Golden Grove 'neath Grongar' is praised by the Rev. Eli Jenkins in his verses in praise of Llaregyb.
[*UMW*, 25].
Map 9 (p. 104).

*Gorseinon, West Glam.*
A small industrial town in the Swansea area.
'he tried to slouch like a newshawk even when he was attending a meeting of the Gorseinon Buffalos', says the Narrator of Thomas the young journalist.
['Return Journey', *CS*, 321].
Map 9 (p. 104).

*Gorslas, Dyfed*
Where Mrs Rose Cottage's sister lives with her twins and their troublesome teeth.
[*UMW*, 40].
Map 9 (p. 104).

*Gwaun-cae-Gurwen, West Glam.*
Where Thomas says he is about to take part in amateur dramatics.
[*CL*, 63: to Pamela Hansford Johnson (prob. early December 1933)].
Map 9 (p. 104).

*Gwili, Dyfed*
One of the rivers listed in the Rev. Eli Jenkins's verses in praise of Llaregyb.
[*UMW*, 25].

*Johnstown, Dyfed*
'The Poplars', Johnstown, was the birthplace, in 1876, of Dylan's father, David John Thomas.
(a) Where Grandpa takes young Thomas for a walk.
(b) The villagers gather in the square to search for the old man.
['A Visit to Grandpa's', *Portrait*, *CS*, 139, 141].
Map 9 (p. 104).

*Kidwelly, Dyfed*
(i) The name of Captain Tiny Evans's ship.
['Quite Early One Morning', *CS*, 294].
(ii) Hermione's uncle Morgan was one of 'the Kidwelly Morgans'.
['The Followers', *CS*, 336].
(iii) The *S.S. Kidwelly* was Captain Cat's old ship.
[*UMW*, 3].
Map 9 (p. 104).

*Lampeter, Dyfed*
During 1941 Thomas sometimes stayed at the Castle Hotel when down from London to visit Caitlin at Talsarn.
Map 9 (p. 104).

*Langower*
See *Llanddowror, Dyfed*, below.

*Llanddowror, Dyfed*
'Langower' is where the dragoons hope to apprehend the rioters.
[*Rebecca's Daughters*, 65].

*Llanelly, Dyfed*
(i) In Llanelly, says Mr Roberts facetiously, turning a glass upside-down was an invitation to a fight.
['Where Tawe Flows', *Portrait*, *CS*, 184].
(ii) 'these women, with the shabby faces and the comedians' tongues . . . might have lurched in from Llanelly on a football night, on the arms of short men with leeks'.
['Four Lost Souls', *ST*, *CS*, 285].
Map 9 (p. 104).

## Llangadock, Dyfed

'The ground is comfy in Llangadock; you can twitch your legs without putting them in the sea'.

['A Visit to Grandpa's, *Portrait*, *CS*, 142. See also, 140].

## Llangain, Dyfed

Thomas's mother's family — the Williamses — came from near this small village between Carmarthen and Llanstephan. Strong family connections persisted throughout Thomas's life; as a boy and a young man he visited frequently, often to stay. His memories of the area inspired some of his finest writing.

See also, *Llanybri*, below.

## Blaen Cwm

A pair of cottages near Llwyn Gwyn (north of the B4312 between Llangain and Llanstephan) owned by the Williams family.

Thomas stayed here as a young man: during September / October 1933 he wrote a number of *Notebook* poems here, including early versions of 'My hero bares his nerves' and 'In the beginning', both of which were published — revised — in *18 Poems* (see *Notebooks*, 236–41, 254–5).

In 1941 Thomas's parents inherited one of the cottages and moved here from Bishopston. Dylan and family stayed during the summers of 1944 and 1945.

*Letters:*

(i) 'a rat-infested cottage in the

*Blaen Cwm*

116

heart of Wales'.

[*CL*, 29: to Pamela Hansford Johnson (late October 1933)].

(ii) A strange, haunting description of walking at night from Blaen Cwm to Llanstephan.

[*CL*, 43-4: to Pamela Hansford Johnson (early November 1933)].

(iii) 'a breeding-box in a cabbage valley'.

[*CL*, 557: to Oscar Williams (30 July 1945). See also, 558].

*Edwinsford Arms*
A pub near Llangain, now closed.

*Letter:*
'a sabbath-dark bar with a stag's head over the Gents'.

[*CL*, 560: to Oscar Williams (30 July 1945)].

*Work:*
Where Grandpa and young Thomas call during their ride from Johnstown to Llanstephan.

['A Visit to Grandpa's', *Portrait*, *CS*, 140].

*Fern Hill*
Really 'Fernhill' (one word). This is a small farm about ¾ mile from Llangain (½ mile past Llangain on B4312 to Llanstephan turn right, then about ¼ mile). It was farmed by Ann Jones and her husband Jim. She was Thomas's Aunt Annie, his mother's eldest sister. She died in Carmarthen Infirmary on 7 February 1933, aged 70.

See *Llanybri*, below.

Two of his most famous poems, 'After the Funeral (In Memory of Ann Jones)' and 'Fern Hill' and the opening *Portrait* story, 'The Peaches', are set wholly or mainly at Fernhill farm.

*Letter:*
'the cancered aunt on her insanitary farm', writes Thomas as she lay dying.

[*CL*, 13: to Trevor Hughes (February 1933)].

*Works:*
(i) The farm — here called 'Gorse-hill' — is the setting of most of the story. 'Gwilym' is based on the Joneses' son Idris.

['The Peaches', *Portrait*, *CS*, 122-37].

(ii) Thomas celebrates his aunt as a representative of traditional Welsh rural life. He describes her funeral and parts of the farm-house.

['After the Funeral', *PDJ*, 136-7; *Notebooks*, 168].

(iii) In his most famous poem Thomas recalls boyhood holidays in the 'lilting house', with Fernhill in the early morning:
    'like a wanderer white
    With the dew'.
The poem is a rhapsodic cele-bration of childhood and of place.

['Fern Hill', *PDJ*, 195-6].

Map 9 (p. 104).

*Fern Hill*

## Llangollen, Clwyd

Thomas visited the International Eisteddfod at Llangollen in July 1953, to write about it for the B.B.C.
'. . . very ordinary . . . Everything is strange. You wish you had a scarlet hat, and bangles, and a little bagpipe to call your own'.
['The International Eisteddfod', *QEOM*, 58-9].

### Castle Street
Down which Thomas walked to see the sights.
['The International Eisteddfod', *QEOM*, 58].
Map 9 (p. 104).

## Llanstephan, Dyfed

(a) Young Thomas and his Grandpa walk from Johnstown into fields near the Llanstephan road.
(b) The pony-cart takes them from Johnstown to Llanstephan village.
['A Visit to Grandpa's', *Portrait*, *CS*, 139-43].

### Churchyard
'There's no sense in lying dead in Llanstephan', considers Grandpa. Llangadock is more comfortable.
['A Visit to Grandpa's', *Portrait*, *CS*, 142. See also, 140].

### Sticks
The wood between Llanstephan Castle and the village.
(i) Possibly referred to in Thomas's description of the raven coughing in 'winter sticks'.
['Especially when the October wind', *PDJ*, 98].
(ii) Where young Thomas and his

Grandpa sit.
['A Visit to Grandpa's', *Portrait*, *CS*, 140].
Map 9 (p. 104).

## Llanybri, Dyfed

Ann Jones and her husband are buried in the chapel graveyard ('Annie Jones, Mount Pleasant, Llangain . . . Also her husband James Jones . . . 'is a translation of part of the Welsh inscription).
See *Llangain*, above.

## Llanybydder, Dyfed

Close by, at Glan Rhyd y Gwiail, Gwilym Thomas (1834-79) was born. This Unitarian minister, school-teacher, and poet, was Dylan's great-uncle. His bardic title, 'Marles', after the Marlais stream near his birthplace, was the source of Dylan's middle name.
Map 9 (p. 104).

## Llyfnant, Dyfed

The river, 'with its waterfall', is praised by the Rev. Eli Jenkins in his verses in praise of Llaregyb.
[*UMW*, 25].

## Loughor, West Glam.

On the outing to Porthcawl 'Jenkins Loughor' was prone to aggressive behaviour if economics was discussed.
['A Story', *CS*, 339].

## Maerdy, Mid Glam.

Known as 'Little Moscow' because of its

119

extreme left-wing politics.
'Little Moscow' is the nickname of a singing drunk from the Valleys.
['Old Garbo', *Portrait, CS*, 213].

*Maesgwyn, Dyfed*
A farm between Llangain and Llanybri.
'Who milks the cows in Maesgwyn?' asks Fourth Drowned.
[*UMW*, 6].

*Merthyr, Mid Glam.*
'Down . . . you bald girls from Merthyr', cries Mr Rafe as he slashes at the grass.
['The Holy Six', *CS*, 101].
Map 9 (p. 104).

*Milford Haven, Dyfed*
Young Thomas remembers old men at the fair 'smelling of Milford Haven in the rain'.
['Holiday Memory', *CS*, 309].
Map 9 (p. 104).

*Moel yr Wyddfa, Gwynedd*
Celebrated in the Rev. Eli Jenkins's verses in praise of Llaregyb].
*UMW*, 24].

*Neath, West Glam.*
*Letter:*
'Come back to Wales in the Neath of adversity', Thomas urges his London-based friend.
[*CL*, 18: to Trevor Hughes (May 1933)].
*Works:*
(i)   One of the towns 'roaring with temp-

tation' visited by Gwilym during a religious tour on which, he said, he met many actresses.
['The Peaches', *Portrait, CS*, 128].
(ii)   Where Mrs Lewis went to look for the erring Mr Roberts.
['Patricia, Edith, and Arnold', *Portrait, CS*, 144].
(iii)   Unable to find a seat, Samuel Bennet occupies the train's toilet from Neath to Paddington.
['A Fine Beginning', *ST, CS*, 248].
Map 9 (p. 104).

*Nedd, West Glam.*
The river Neath, listed in the Rev. Eli Jenkins's verses in praise of Llaregyb.
[*UMW*, 25].

*Newport, Gwent*
One of the towns 'roaring with temptation', visited by Gwilym during a religious tour on which, he said, he met many actresses.
['The Peaches', *Portrait, CS*, 128].
Map 9 (p. 104).

*New Quay, Dyfed*
A small coastal town of fishermen and tourists. From September 1944 to early summer 1945 the Thomases lived nearby.
*Letters:*
(i)   A place that he will soon leave for London.
[*CL*, 524: verse-letter to T. W. Earp (21 September 1944). This section is not in *PDJ*, 179].
(ii)   'though it is lovely here I am not'.
[*CL*, 553 (21 May 1945)].

*Works:*
(i) The subject of one of Thomas's verse-
letters.
['New Quay', *PDJ*, 179 (for a longer
version see *SL*, 267-8)].
(ii) The setting and subject of the story.
['Quite Early One Morning', *CS*,
291].
(iii) 'the toppling town'.
['The Crumbs of One Man's Year',
*CS*, 314].
(iv) Llaregyb is *partly* based on New
Quay.
[*UMW*, *passim*. See also, 'Quite Early
One Morning', *CS*, 294-5].

*Beach*
'the wild, umbrella'd, and french
lettered Beach.'
['New Quay', *PDJ*, 179].

*Bethel Chapel, Margaret Street*
'Mr Jones the Cake' is a 'Bethel-
worm' who 'minces among knickers'.
['New Quay', *PDJ*, 179].

*Black Lion Hotel, Glamorgan Terrace*
Where Thomas was a regular.
(i) Thomas complained that the pub
only sold:
'Buckley's unfrisky
Mild'.
'Buckley's' is a beer made in
Llanelli.
['New Quay', *PDJ*, 179].
(ii) The 'pink-washed pub' that
waits for Saturday night is
probably the 'Black Lion'.
['Quite Early One Morning',
*CS*, 291].
(iii) Where a cat could be found and

*Black Lion*

*Majoda*

'gently swilling retired sea-captains in the snug-as-a-bug back bar'.
['The Crumbs of One Man's Year', *CS*, 314].

*Cloth Hall*
Unidentified.
The milkman dreams of the sound of choirs rising past it.
['Quite Early One Morning', *CS*, 291].

*Cross Inn*
Three miles from New Quay on the A486.
Where a creeping drinker fouls the beds.
['A Pub Poem', *PDJ*, 242].

*Harbour*
The quay is still 'shouldering out'. The grey warehouse adjacent to the harbour pier is no longer empty but houses harbour offices and the New Quay Yacht Club.
['Quite Early One Morning', *CS*, 291].

*King's Head*
Unidentified.
Where whistling Phoebe is the maid.
['Quite Early One Morning', *CS*, 294].

*Majoda*
A tiny bungalow with magnificent sea-views where the Thomases lived during their stay in New Quay. 'Majoda' is about 1 mile from the

*New Quay Harbour*

town, a few hundred yards down a left turn off the Aberaeron road opposite the Cambrian Hotel.
(i) 'this wood-and-asbestos pagoda'.
  [*CL*, 520: verse-letter to T. W. Earp (1 September 1944)].
(ii) 'a shack at the edge of the cliff where my children hop like fleas in a box'.
  [*CL*, 551: to Oscar Williams (28 March 1945)].

*Manchester House, Margaret Street*
The milkman dreams of the sound of choirs rising past it.
['Quite Early One Morning', *CS*, 291].

*Police-Station*
One, wrote Thomas, it had a forbidding roof. New Quay no longer has a police-station.

['Quite Early One Morning', *CS*, 291].

*St Ina's Church*
At Llanina, 1 mile across the bay, is the 'splashed' church.
['Quite Early One Morning', *CS*, 291].

*Towyn Welsh Congregational Chapel*
A chapel with a 'cold long eye' (i.e. a long, thin and prominent end window).
['Quite Early One Morning', *CS*, 293. See also, 291].
Map 9 (p. 104).

*North Wales*
An area almost unknown to Thomas.
*Letter:*
From Harlech North Wales is 'just a bit further on, one way or the other'.

[*CL*, 309: to Henry Treece (6/7 July 1938)].
*Work:*
Where Llangollen was.
['The International Eisteddfod', *QEOM*, 58].


*Ogmore, Mid Glam.*
'Celebrated' in Mr Ogmore, first husband of Mrs Ogmore-Pritchard.
[*UMW*, 14-16, 31, 38-41, 44-5, 52, 76-8]. Map 9 (p. 104).

*Ogwr, Mid Glam.*
The river Ogmore. Listed in the Rev. Eli Jenkins's verses in praise of Llaregyb.
[*UMW*, 25].

*Pembroke, Dyfed*
(i) (a) A vampire with a scissors is a devil from Pembroke, thinks Mrs Price the midwife.
(b) The narrator urges Pembroke to sleep well because the devils have left.
['The School for Witches', *CS*, 67, 70].
(ii) (a) Where the chaise is going in the opening sequence.
(b) Where much of the action takes place.
[*'Rebecca's Daughters'*, 8-9, 22, 30, 34, 55, 71, 116].
(iii) Where Mr Waldo lived near the 'Castle Keep', worked as a chimney sweep, and had amorous — though sooty — adventures.
[*UMW*, 83].
Map 9 (p. 104).

*St Ina's*

*Pembrokeshire, Dyfed*
The setting.
[*Rebecca's Daughters, passim*].


*Pendine Sands, Dyfed*
Where the grammar-school boys wished to drive fast cars.
['The Fight', *Portrait, CS*, 155].
Map 9 (p. 104).


*Penmaenmawr, Gwynedd*
Celebrated by the Rev. Eli Jenkins in his verses in praise of Llaregyb.
[*UMW*, 25].


*Plinlimmon, Dyfed*
'. . . old in story', says the Rev. Eli Jenkins in his verses in praise of Llaregyb.
[*UMW*, 24].


*Pont-Neath-Vaughan, West Glam.*
Where Samuel Bennet's Auntie Morgan came from.
['Four Lost Souls', *ST, CS*, 284].
Map 9 (p. 104).


*Porth, Mid Glam.*
'London is good; Porth is better'.
[*CL*, 184: to Bert Trick (prob. February 1935)].
Map.


*Porthcawl, Mid Glam.*
A South Wales seaside resort.
(i) Where the Narrator's friends are spending Saturday night.

['One Warm Saturday', *Portrait, CS*, 221].
(ii) Jean thinks Mewslade is 'nicer than Porthcawl'.
['Extraordinary Little Cough', *Portrait, CS*, 171].
(iii) Where the Bennets got their toast-rack.
['A Fine Beginning', *ST, CS*, 242].
(iv) In New Quay a water-colour of Porthcawl can be found in bedrooms above the alarm-clocks.
['Quite Early One Morning', *CS*, 292].
(v) Where Hetty's Uncle Eliot died of cramp.
['The Followers', *CS*, 335].
(vi) (a) Where the outing is going.
(b) Where Uncle believes it will arrive.
(c) The river in which the outing ends is, the men consider, better.
['A Story', *CS*, 337, 339, 343].

*Coney Beach*
The pleasure park to which the Narrator's friends took girls and where Leslie Bird won coconuts.
['One Warm Saturday', *Portrait, CS*, 221].

*Esplanade Hotel*
Where Molly is bought a drink with a cherry in it.
['One Warm Saturday', *Portrait, CS*, 221].

*Promenade*
Through the lounge window the sun can be viewed sinking over the Promenade.
['One Warm Saturday', *Portrait, CS*, 221].
Map 9 (p. 104).

*Pembroke*

126

*Radnorshire, Powys*
The 'Spirit of Poetry' celebrates beautiful Radnorshire gum-trees.
['Spajma and Salnady', *EP*, 141].


*Red Roses, Dyfed*
'Rhos Goch' in Welsh. Rebecca's daughters meet here.
[*Rebecca's Daughters*, 123, 129, 131-2].


*Rhondda, Mid Glam.*
*Letter:*
Thomas described his new poem as 'a kind of colloquial Lycidas set in the Rhondda Valley'.
[*CL*, 721: to John Davenport (prob. late 1949)].
*Work:*
Where Cedric, the fashionable and socially-concerned poet, considers spending a holiday to sample 'real life', but does not.
['How to be a Poet', *Prospect*, 112].
Map 9 (p. 104).


*St Clear's, Dyfed*
Where Anthony Raine and Rhiannon are stopped at the toll-gate.
[*Rebecca's Daughters*, 26].
Map 9 (p. 104).


*Sawdde, Dyfed*
A river listed in the Rev. Eli Jenkins's verses in praise of Llaregyb.
[*UMW*, 25].


*Senny, Powys*
A river listed in the Rev. Eli Jenkins's

verses in praise of Llaregyb.
[*UMW*, 25].


*Skewen, West Glam.*
Where Thomas, the young journalist, reported a rehearsal of *The Mikado*.
['Return Journey', *CS*, 321].
Map 9 (p. 104).

*South Wales*
Part of the address that young Thomas writes in his reporter's note-book.
['Old Garbo', *Portrait*, *CS*, 210].


*Taf, Dyfed*
Laugharne is on its estuary.
'. . . . full tilt river . . .
   . . . the livelong river'.
['Poem on his Birthday', *PDJ*, 208-9].


*Taff, Mid Glam.*
The river that flows through Cardiff. Praised as 'broad and free' in the Rev. Eli Jenkins's verses celebrating Llaregyb.
[*UMW*, 25].


*Talsarn, Dyfed*
During Summer 1942 Caitlin and Llewellyn stayed here with friends at 'Gelli', Talsarn. Thomas visited frequently from London. Talsarn is on the river Aeron after which the Thomases' daughter Aeron(wy) is named. She was, said her parents, conceived at Talsarn.
'I tossed off this morning over Talsarn Bridge to the fishes,' Thomas writes, improbably, from 'Gelli'.

[*CL*, 501: to T. W. Earp (30 August 1942)].
Map 9 (p. 104).

*Templeton, Dyfed*
Through which the police march on their way from London to Pembroke.
[*Rebecca's Daughters*, 70-1].

*Tenby, Dyfed*
In October 1953 — within weeks of his death in New York — Thomas gave a solo reading of *Under Milk Wood* to the Tenby Arts Club.
Map 9 (p. 104).

*Tintern, Gwent*
Wordsworth's poem is mentioned by George Ring, who then argues with a man in the 'Gayspot' Club whose sister is a waitress in Tintern.
['Four Lost Souls', *ST*, *CS*, 286].
Map 9 (p. 104).

*Tonypandy, Mid Glam.*
The 'distant and improbable' place where some inhabitants of Laugharne used to live.
['Laugharne', *QEOM*, 70].
Map 9 (p. 104).

*Towy, Dyfed*
Llanstephan is on the river's estuary.
(i) Young Thomas aims sling-shots at Towy gulls.
['A Visit to Grandpa's', *Portrait*, *CS*, 140].
(ii) Observed from above. The heron goes fishing in 'the tear of the Towy'.
['Over Sir John's Hill', *PDJ*, 203. See also, 201-2].

(iii) Praised as 'broad and free' in the Rev. Eli Jenkins's verses celebrating Llaregyb.
[*UMW*, 25].

*Trecynon, Mid Glam.*
Where Thomas acted with the Little Theatre.
[*CL*, 48: to Pamela Hansford Johnson (c. 11 November 1933)].
Map 9 (p. 104).

*Treorchy, Mid Glam.*
Home of the Fat Man.
['After the Fair', *CS* 2].
Map 9 (p. 104).

*Twll*
A joke: the word is Welsh for 'hole'.
Where Mog Edwards had a draper's shop.
[*UMW*, 49].

*Valleys*
A general term for the inland, coal-mining valleys of South Wales.
(i) 'Valley children, with sunken, impudent eyes', play on Swansea sands.
['One Warm Saturday', *Portrait*, *CS*, 220].
(ii) (a) In the crowds along Swansea's High Street are men from the Valleys in town to watch football.
(b) Mr Farr sneers at young men flirting with the 'Carlton' barmaid as 'Toop little Twms from the Valleys' for whom, he predicts, vomiting is imminent.
['Old Garbo', *Portrait*, *CS*, 207, 213].

*Talsarn*

(iii) In Paddington Station buffet Samuel Bennet sees a man who might be 'a deacon from the Valleys on a mean blind, with his pocket-book sewn in his combs'.
['A Fine Beginning', *Portrait*, *CS*, 255].

(iv) Into the 'Marlborough' pub come 'Men from the valleys . . . for nine or ten' pints of beer.
['The Followers', *CS*, 331].

*West Wales*
(i) Which smoked and sent up cries to God.
['The Horse's Ha', *CS*, 59. See also, 61].
(ii) Which moved in its grave.
['The School for Witches', *CS*, 65].

*Whitland, Dyfed*
Sir Henry Price-Parry and Anthony Raine are directors of the Whitland Turnpike Trust.
[*Rebecca's Daughters*, 38].
Map 9 (p. 104).

# CHAPTER FIVE

# LONDON

## 'city of the restless dead'

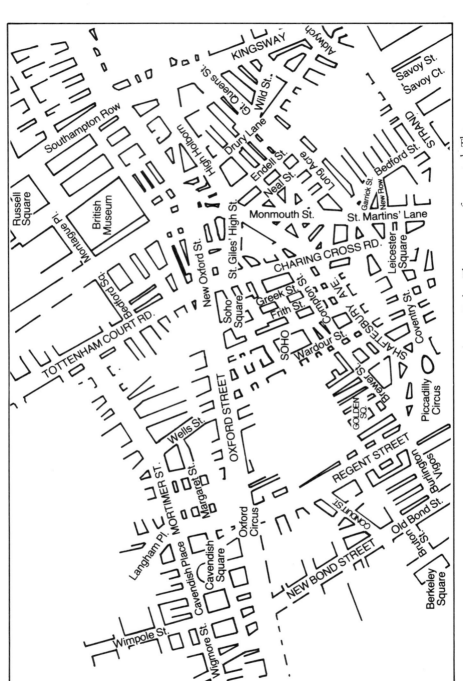

*Note:* The above map refers to the streets and areas Dylan Thomas most frequented. The reader is advised to use *Geographers London A–Z Street Atlas* for other roads and streets.

Although Dylan Thomas was only 18 when he first visited London during August 1933, he had already published work in metropolitan magazines: the famous 'And death shall have no dominion' appeared in the *New English Weekly* of 18 May 1933. For at least part of that first visit he stayed at Chertsey with his married sister Nancy but quickly made contacts within literary circles. From 1934 to the end of his life he either lived in the city or visited frequently.

London was another crucial place. Within two years of his first visit the publication of *18 Poems* made him a literary celebrity and he had begun to relish that role in the pubs and clubs of the capital. London made him and then, with cruel adroitness, began to destroy him.

The following works, either wholly or in part, have recognizable 'London' settings:

(a) *Poems*
'The Countryman's Return'
'Deaths and Entrances'
'Among those Killed in the Dawn Raid was a Man Aged a Hundred'
'Ceremony after a Fire Raid'
'A Refusal to Mourn the Death, by Fire, of a Child in London'
'Holy Spring'

(b) *Fiction*
*Adventures in the Skin Trade*
'The Crumbs of One Man's Year'

(c) *Other Writings*
'Our Country'
'The English Festival of Spoken Poetry'
'How to be a Poet'
'The Festival Exhibition, 1951'

## Letters

(i)     In London, writes the youthful Thomas to the girl he is now in love with, he will soon find 'a high, conventional garret, there to invoke the sadistic Muses, get a little drunk on air'.
[*CL*, 123: to Pamela Hansford Johnson (2 May 1934)].

(ii)     As a hard-drinker who loved to offend polite society Thomas allows his Swansea friend a glimpse of self-doubt: 'All London is out of step, except me'.
[*CL*, 184: to Bert Trick (prob. February 1935)].

(iii)     Thomas is recuperating in Cornwall from a visit to a London full of 'promiscuity, booze, coloured shirts, too much talk, too little work'.
[*CL*, 222 (c. 20 April 1936)].

(iv)     To Ringwood, Hampshire, where Caitlin waits for the birth of their first son, Thomas has recently returned from his 'city of the restless dead . . . its glamour smells of goat; there's no difference between good & bad'.
[*CL*, 343 (20 December 1938)].

(v)     Again back in Ringwood, with Caitlin still waiting, Thomas has been to London to meet Henry Miller and Lawrence Durrell. They spent two days together in 'nightmare London', talking a lot and drinking even more.
[*CL*, 351 (c. 8 January 1939)].

(vi)     With the War raging Caitlin and Dylan are penniless and, as yet, homeless, in 'stinking, friendless London'.
[*CL*, 493 (28 August 1941)].

(vii)     To the Welsh woman whom he had met through his work for Strand films Thomas confesses that in London, without her, 'even the sun's grey and God how I hate it'.
[*CL*, 496: to (Ruth Wynn Owen) (prob. May 1942)].

(viii) From New Quay, to which he has just returned, Thomas writes, of London, that he 'hated it more than ever'.
[*CL*, 553 (21 May 1945)].

(ix)     For John Davenport, see Chapter Six / *Marshfield*. Thomas reports from Laugharne on a recent visit to the metropolis: 'occasional agitated bumbling in frowsy streets, unkind pubs, deleterious afternoon boozers, snoring cinemas, wet beds'.
[*CL*, 793: to John Davenport (12 April 1951)].

(x)     Donald Taylor produced films for which Thomas wrote scripts in vain attempts to keep wolves from doors in 'creditless London'.

[*CL*, 804: to Donald Taylor (31 August 1951)].

(xi)  For 'Princess Caetani', see Chapter Three / Letter ix. One excuse for not finishing *Under Milk Wood* for her magazine is because Thomas had spent some time in 'London, which, to me, is nowhere'.
[*CL*, 845: to Margerite Caetani (6 November 1952)].


## *Works*

(i)  'the wind . . .
To London's turned'.
['With windmills turning wrong directions', *PDJ*, 37; *Notebooks*, 346].

(ii)  The girl cut bread so thinly that she could see London through each piece.
['The Orchards', *CS*, 47].

(iii)  In the doctor's tower a sign points to London.
['The Lemon', *CS*, 56].

(iv)  After Dan Jenkyn has listened to the poem young Thomas feels the 'future spread out beyond the window . . . and into smoky London paved with poems'.
['The Fight', *Portrait*, *CS*, 159].

(v)  (a) Where young Mr Thomas soon hoped to live.
(b) Where Mr Roberts had stayed.
(c) In Mr Evans's contribution to the friends' novel, *Where Tawe Flows*, John William Hughes is a former London draper retired to Cardiganshire.
['Where Tawe Flows', *Portrait*, *CS*, 181, 184, 192].

(vi)  Where George Gray of Norfolk Street, Swansea, used to live.
['Who Do You Wish Was With Us?', *Portrait*, *CS*, 204].

(vii)  'low-faluting
London . . .
. . . the hypnotised city'.
['The Countryman's Return', *PDJ*, 154, 156].

(viii) One of the places that seem like 'cobbles' in the rural tide.
['Ballad of the Long-Legged Bait', *PDJ*, 168].

(ix)  (a) ' "I don't know where I'm going . . . That's why I came up to London", ' says Samuel Bennet to Mr Allingham.
(b) Samuel's London is a city of 'knickerless women enamouring from the cane tables, waiting in the fumes for the country cousins to stagger in, all savings and haywisps'.
['A Fine Beginning', *ST*, *CS*, 254; 'Four Lost Souls', *ST*, *CS*, 284. See also: *CS*, 251, 253, 260, 261, 271, 278, 285].

(x)     A waking man stares at the city's wheels.
        ['A Dream of Winter', *The Doctor and the Devils and Other Scripts*, 208].
(xi)    When he was young, Thomas recalls, beyond Wales was 'England which
        was London'.
        ['Reminiscences of Childhood (Second Version)', QEOM, 9].
(xii)   'the dumb, heroic streets
        . . . the ten-million-headed city'.
        ['Our Country', *QEOM (USA)*, 90, 91].
(xiii)  'the altar of London'.
        ['Ceremony after a Fire Raid', PDJ, 174].
(xiv)   The narrator recalls spring in London and a disillusioning bus journey.
        ['The Crumbs of One Man's Year', CS, 313].
(xv)    Advice on how to begin a story is as free as — and less smuttier than — the
        air in London.
        ['How to begin a Story', QEOM, 38].
(xvi)   Passer-By recalls young Thomas and his friends looking forward to the
        time when they would 'ring the bells of London and paint it like a tart'.
        ['Return Journey', CS, 322. See also, 323].
(xvii)  The venue of
        ['The English Festival of Spoken Poetry', QEOM, 127].
(xviii) Extra police travel from London to Pembrokeshire to help quell the
        Rebecca riots.
        [*Rebecca's Daughters*, 66, 69. See also, 49].
(xix)   Where Welsh artists sometimes anglicize themselves out of existence.
        ['Wales and the Artist', QEOM, 153].
(xx)    Where poets make careers and find fame.
        ['How to be a Poet', *Prospect*, 104-15].
(xxi)   'the Capital punishment . . . the huge petty misshaped nightmare'. Such,
        initially, seemed the venue for
        ['The Festival Exhibition, 1951', QEOM, 53, 57].

*Antelope, Edgeware Road, W.2*
Samuel Bennet drinks with Mr Allingham
and friends in the saloon bar, and meets
three giggling young women.
['Four Lost Souls', *ST*, *CS*, 278-9].

*Antelope Hotel, Sloane Square, S.W.1*
A favourite Thomas pub; it 'drawled with
moustaches'.
[*CL*, 513: to T. W. Earp (prob. February
1944)].

*Barnes, S.W.13*
Alfred is an expert on pubs from Shepherds Bush to Barnes.
['The Londoner', *The Doctor and the Devils
and Other Scripts*, 216].

*53 Battersea Rise, S.W.11*
Here, with her widowed mother, lived
Pamela Hansford Johnson. She was two
years older than Thomas and wrote to him
when his poem, 'That sanity be kept'
appeared in the *Sunday Referee* (3 September 1933). They corresponded, visited
each other's homes, and almost married.
Thereafter she became a novelist of
quality. In 1950 she married C. P. (later
Lord) Snow, the scientist and distinguished novelist.

*Bedford Street, W.C.2*
J. M. Dent & Sons Ltd, Thomas's British
publishers, were at Aldine House. Pearn,
Pollinger and Higham (later David
Higham Associates), his literary agents,

*Battersea Rise*

137

were at 39–40.
Map 10 (p. 132).

*Billingsgate, E.C.3*
The old fish-market that has given its name to foul-mouthed speech has, Thomas considers, become part of our priceless linguistic heritage.
['Idioms', *EP*, 163].

*Bloomsbury, W.C.1*
Thomas always saw himself reacting against 'Bloomsbury' writers (of whom Virginia Woolf was the most talented and famous).
*Letters:*
(i) A production of *The Duchess of Malfi* is despised as 'Bloomsbury aesthetish'.

[*CL*, 184: to Bert Trick (prob. February 1935)].
(ii) 'Let's . . . stamp up Bloomsbury, waving our cocks'.
[*CL*, 207: to Rayner Heppenstall (31 December 1935)].
*Work:*
Bloomsbury, says Mr Evans, is where the 'neurotic poets' live.
['Where Tawe Flows', *Portrait, CS*, 188].
Map 10 (p. 132).

*British Museum, W.C.1*
One of the tourist attractions mentioned by Mr Allingham when he first meets Samuel Bennet in Paddington Station buffet.
['A Fine Beginning', *ST. CS*, 251].
Map 10 (p. 132).

*Cafe Royale — Back Bar*

*Café Royal, 68 Regent Street, W.1.*
Thomas drank regularly in the back bar:
'the royal back-bar of beyond'.
[*CL*, 506: verse-letter to T. W. Earp (1 July 1943)].
Map 10 (p. 132).

*Chelsea, S.W.3*
To aspiring provincials in the 1930s 'Chelsea' suggested glamorous literary life.
*Letter:*
A disappointing place of 'shabby drunkenness'.
[*CL*, 208: to Rayner Heppenstall (31 December 1935)].
*Works:*
(i)   Where Mrs Wigmore gave artistic parties.

['The Sincerest Form of Flattery', *EP*, 91].
(ii)   Young Thomas would soon be leaving for Chelsea, where he 'hoped, in a vague way, to live on women'.
['Where Tawe Flows', *Portrait*, *CS*, 181].

*Chelsea Reach, S.W.3*
Used to rhyme with 'tricks of speech'.
[*CL*, 68: letter, partly in verse, to Pamela Hansford Johnson (late 1933)].

*Chertsey*
For at least part of his first visit to London

*Dean Street*

139

in August 1933, Thomas stayed with his sister Nancy and her first husband, Haydn Taylor, who were living in a houseboat on the Thames.

## 21 Coleherne Road, S.W.10
Thomas lived here, briefly, during 1935.

## Crouch End, N.8
Where Lucy Wakefield's man came from. ['Four Lost Souls', *ST*, *CS*, 285].

## Crystal Palace, S.E.19
Where, said Mr Allingham, there would be space for dancing.

['Four Lost Souls', *ST*, *CS*, 289].

## Dean Street, Soho, W.1
'Beardlessly wagging in Dean Street'. ['The Countryman's Return', *PDJ*, 156]. See also, *The French Pub* and *Gargoyle Club*, below.
Map 10 (p. 132).

## 54 Delancey Street, Camden Town, N.W.1
The property was owned by Thomas's patron, Margaret Taylor, first wife of A. J. P. Taylor. Dylan, Caitlin and family lived in the basement flat from October 1951 to 20 January 1952, before returning to the Boat House at Laugharne. A Blue Plaque — the only one relating to Thomas

*54 Delancey Street*

— now commemorates their stay.

'our new London house or horror on bus and nightlorry route and opposite railway bridge and shunting station. No herons here.'
[*CL*, 818: to John Malcolm Brinnin (3 December 1951)].

*10 Downing Street, S.W.1*
Where Sir John Watkyn speaks up for the rioters.
[*Rebecca's Daughters*, 118].

*Duke of York's Pub, 47 Rathbone Street, W.1*
Here, on one occasion, Thomas felt like 'a piece of cold lamb with vomit sauce'.
[*CL*, 618: to T. W. Earp (1 March 1947)].
Map 10 (p. 132).

*Edgware Road, W.2*
'I'm dancing with three strangers down Edgware Road in the rain, cried Samuel'.
['Four Lost Souls', *ST*, *CS*, 278. See also, 277].

*Fitzroy Tavern, Charlotte Street, W.1*
The heart of 'Fitzrovia', the London literary world of the 1930s, and a favourite Thomas pub.
Map 10 (p. 132).

*Fleet Street, E.C.4*
(i) Fleet Street nature-writers play flutes for goats, wrote the adolescent Thomas somewhat mysteriously.
['With all the fever of the August months', *Notebooks*, 173].
(ii) Where Ted Williams, young Thomas's colleague on the *Tawe News*, dreams of being.
['Old Garbo', *Portrait*, *CS*, 210].

*The French House, 49 Dean Street, Soho, W.1*
Much frequented by Thomas, this pub's correct name was the 'York Minster'. In 1983 it was officially renamed 'The French House'.
Map 10 (p. 132).

*Frisco's, 17 Frith Street, W.1*
Its real name was the 'International Bar'. 'Frisco' was the proprietor's nickname. This night-club, sometimes used by Thomas, was blitzed and removed to various subsequent addresses (40 Sackville Street, W.1; 25 Curzon Street, W.1; 33 Shepherd Market, W.1). It closed in the year of Thomas's death.
Map 10 (p. 132).

*Gargoyle Club, 69 Dean Street, Soho, W.1*
Thomas was a regular at this drinking-club owned by his friend David Tennant. It occupied the upper floors of 69 Dean Street and has long been defunct. The building is now offices.
Map 10 (p. 132).

*Fitzroy Tavern*

*The French Pub, York Minster*

*Gargoyle Club*

*The George, Langham Place, W.1*
This pub is called the 'Gluepot' (a nick-name said to have been coined by Sir Thomas Beecham when referring to the difficulty of getting his musicians out of it). Thomas was a regular here when working for the B.B.C.
Map 10 (p. 132).

*1 Golden Square, W.1*
Once the headquarters of Donald Taylor's Strand Film Company Ltd. During the war Thomas wrote scripts for Taylor in an office full of 'repressed women . . . punishing typewriters, and queers in striped suits talking about "cinema".'
[*CL*, 497: to (Ruth Wynn Owen) (prob. May 1942)].
Map 10 (p. 132).

*7 Great Ormond Street, W.C.1*
Here were the offices of Europa Press, who agreed to publish *The Burning Baby: 16 Stories* in 1938. The Press eventually with-drew, fearing prosecution for obscenity.
Map 10 (p. 132).

*Hammersmith, W.6*
Where Lily met Ted Jackson in a dance-hall.
['The Londoner', *The Doctor and the Devils and Other Scripts*, 224].

*13 Hammersmith Terrace, W.6*
The Thomases lived here in late 1941 in a studio owned by A. P. Herbert. Only a few doors away was Caitlin's birthplace

*The George, Langham Place*

(8 December 1913).

*Hampstead, N.W.3*
Where, Thomas always considered, was located an effete yet powerful literary establishment.
'. . . nostalgic Hampstead . . . full of the soft cries of reviewers and the gentle choosing of books'.
[*CL*, 327: to John Davenport (23 September 1938)].

*Harrow*
Where Thomas stayed with Daniel Jones during 1935.
See also, *Rayner's Lane*, below.

*Harrow on the Hill*
One of the sensible places.
['The first ten years in school and park', *Notebooks*, 193].

*Helvetia, 23 Old Compton Street, Soho, W.1*
A pub sometimes used by Thomas. In October 1953, shortly before leaving for his final visit to America, he lost the manuscript of *Under Milk Wood*. Douglas Cleverden, the B.B.C. producer, was told by Thomas that if he found it he could keep it. Cleverden found it in the 'Helvetia'.
Map 10 (p. 132).

*Helvetia*

*Horseshoe Club, 21 Wardour Street, W.1*
A drinking-club occasionally used by Thomas. The club has long gone and replaced by a baker's and a life assurance company.
[*CL*, 506: verse-letter to T. W. Earp (1 July 1943)].
Map 10 (p. 132).

*House of Commons, S.W.1*
(i)  A facetious term for the lavatory.
     ['One Warm Saturday', *Portrait*, *CS*, 236; *UMW*, 50].
(ii) Where Sir John Watkyn speaks for Pembrokeshire.
     [*Rebecca's Daughters*, 66].

*Kew Gardens, Richmond*
Where Lily Jackson's bus seemed to go.
['The Londoner', *The Doctor and the Devils and Other Scripts*, 216].

*164 King's Road, Chelsea, S.W.3*
The branch of Lloyds Bank at which Thomas kept his account.

*Ladder Club, 3 & 5 Bruton Place, W.1*
An afternoon drinking-club near Berkeley Square frequented by Thomas. The site is now occupied by R. A. Lee (Fine Arts) Ltd.
[*CL*: 506: verse-letter to T. W. Earp (1 July 1943)].
Map 10 (p. 132).

*Lime Grove Studios, Shepherds Bush, W.12*
Headquarters of Gainsborough Films, for whom, in 1948, Thomas scripted *Rebecca's Daughters*, *The Beach at Falesá* and *Me and My Bike*.

*The Load of Hay, 144 Praed Street, W.2*
A pub near Paddington Station popular with visitors from Wales. It closed in 1970 and the building is now a branch of Garfunkel's Restaurants.
      Samuel Bennet expects to find children from Swansea playing outside.
['A Fine Beginning', *ST*, *CS*, 249].

*National Liberal Club, Whitehall*

*Lord's Cricket Ground, St John's Wood, N.W.8*
Where Thomas watched cricket and drank all day.
Where nobody scored.
['The Londoner', *The Doctor and the Devils and Other Scripts*, 226].

*Mandrake Club, 4 Meard Street, Soho, W.1*
A favourite Thomas haunt during the last

years of his life. Ostensibly a chess–club the Mandrake seems to have been more a drinking-club. The site and much of Meard Street was bombed-out during the early 1980s.
Map 10 (p. 132).

*Manresa Road, Chelsea, S.W.3*
For periods from Autumn 1942 to early 1943 the Thomases lived in Manresa Road at 3 Wentworth Studios (redeveloped). On 3 March 1943 daughter Aeronwy was

146

born in St Mary Abbots Hospital nearby.

*Marble Arch, W.1*
Pointed out by Mr Allingham during a taxi-ride to the 'Gayspot' club.
['Four Lost Souls', *ST, CS*, 282].

*6 Markham Square, King's Road, Chelsea, S.W.3*
Where Caitlin's sister Nicolette lived as the wife of the fashionable painter, Anthony Devas. From time to time the Thomases were their unwelcome guests and, during Autumn 1945, occupied the basement flat.
Map.

*Mecklenburgh Square, W.C.1*
Where a sinister policeman patrolled.
['How to be a Poet', *Prospect*, 110].

*National Liberal Club, Whitehall Place, S.W.1*
Thomas was a member from 1947 to 1949.

*Paddington Station, W.2*
The London terminus for trains from Wales. In 1933 the station was Thomas's first sight of the city.
Samuel Bennet meets Mr Allingham in the station buffet and so begins his London adventures.
['A Fine Beginning', *ST, CS*, 248-57. See

*Paddington Station*

147

also 'Plenty of Furniture', *ST*, *CS*, 265, 272].

### Palmer's Green, N.13
Where Mr Roberts stayed with the Armitages, who sent each other messages on toilet paper.
['Where Tawe Flows', *Portrait*, *CS*, 184].

### Park Lane, W.1
Pointed out by Mr Allingham during the tax-ride to the 'Gayspot' club.
['Four Lost Souls', *ST*, *CS*, 282].

### 68 Parliament Hill, Hampstead, N.W.3
Home of the poet Anna Wickham (Mrs Patrick Hepburn). Thomas stayed here during 1937. Through Anna Wickham he met Lawrence Durrell.

The Hepburn's bathroom, with its caged birds, is used as the setting of Samuel Bennet's amorous and unfortunate adventures in the bath with Polly.
['Plenty of Furniture', *ST*, *CS*, 267ff].

### Piccadilly, W.1
(i) 'The Piccadilly men, the back street drunks'.
['We who are young are old', *PDJ*, 41; *Notebooks*, 171].
(ii) Pointed out by Mr Allingham during the taxi-ride to the 'Gayspot' club.
['Four Lost Souls', *ST*, *CS*, 282, 283].
Map 10 (p. 132).

### Pimlico, S.W.1
Samuel Bennet imagines living in Pimlico with a woman he sees in Paddington

Station buffet.
['A Fine Beginning', *ST*, *CS*, 250].

### Praed Street, W.2
' "This is Praed Street." "It's dull, isn't it?" ' say Mr Allingham and Samuel Bennet, respectively.
['A Fine Beginning', *ST*, *CS*, 257. See also, 'A Fine Beginning', 254; 'Four Lost Souls', *ST*, *CS*, 277].
Map 10 (p. 132).

### Rayner's Lane, Harrow
Thomas's friend, Trevor Hughes, moved from Swansea to Perwell Avenue. Thomas visited him during late Summer 1933.

### 5 Redcliffe Street, Fulham Road, S.W.10
Thomas's first London address: from 10 November 1934 to early 1935 he shared a bedsitter with the Swansea artist, Alfred Janes. The artist Mervyn Levy, also from Swansea, lived elsewhere in the house.
'the quarter of the pseudo–artists, of the beards, of the naughty expressions of an entirely outmoded period of artistic importance'.

[*CL*, 177: to Bert Trick (December 1934)].

### Ritz Hotel, Piccadilly, W.1
' "That's the Ritz. Stop for a kipper, Sam?" ' says Mr Allingham.
['Four Lost Souls', *ST*, *CS*, 282].
Map 10 (p. 132).

### Rossetti Mansions, Flood Street, S.W.3
Where John Davenport lived and where

the Thomases occasionally stayed.

*St Martin's Lane, W.C.2*
Gryphon Films, for whom Thomas wrote
film scripts during the war, was in Guild
House.
Map 10 (p. 132).

*St Paul's Cathedral, E.C.4*
(i)  The cathedral's 'eyes' move over the
city.
['Our Country', *QEOM (USA)*, 90].
(ii) A symbol of permanence.
['The Festival Exhibition, 1951',
*QEOM*, 57].

*27 St Peter's Square, Hammersmith,
W.6*
Norman Cameron's flat, where Thomas
stayed during 1936.

*St Stephen's Hospital, Fulham Road,
S.W.10*
During February or March 1946 Thomas
was admitted for four days with alcoholic
gastritis.

*Savage Club, 1 Carlton House Terrace,
S.W.1 (later at King Street, W.C.2)*
Thomas became a member in March 1949.

*Savoy Hotel, W.C.2*
To which Lou compares the 'Victoria

*Savage Club*

saloon'.
['One Warm Saturday'. *Portrait, CS*, 226].
Map 10 (p. 132).

*Sewell Street*
Unidentified. It's off Praed Street, says
Samuel Bennet; it *could* be Sale Place.
    Where Mr Allingham lives and Samuel
has his adventures in the bath.
['A Fine Beginning', 254, 257; 'Plenty of
Furniture', 268, 271; 'Four Lost Souls', *ST*,
*CS*, 277].

*Shepherds Bush, W.12*
49 Montrose Street, Shepherds Bush, is
the fictitious address of Mr & Mrs Jackson
and so the setting of Thomas's radio script.
['The Londoner', *The Doctor and the Devils*

149

*and Other Scripts*, 213-29].

*Slade Art School, Gower Street, W.C.1*
Hotchkiss, the 'week-ending poet', has 'an ambitious wife . . . who lost the battle of the Slade'.
['How to be a Poet', *Prospect*, 106].

*Soho, W.1*
Where, during the 1930s and 1940s, Thomas was well known in the pubs and clubs.
'I was born in Cwmbwrla, but Soho's better for my *gouaches*', says the anglicized Welsh artist.
['Wales and the Artist', *QEOM*, 153].
Map 10 (p. 132).

*34 Soho Square, W.1*
The Film Centre, frequented by Thomas when writing war-time film-scripts.
Map 10 (p. 132).

*South Bank, S.E.1*
Site of the Festival of Britain.
['The Festival Exhibition, 1951', *QEOM*, 50-7].

*South Kensington, S.W.7*
Where, Mr Allingham tells Samuel Bennet, there is a museum.
['A Fine Beginning', *ST*, *CS*, 251].

*Strand, W.C.2*
A sea-covered Strand is used by Thomas to suggest the unlikely.

*Swiss Tavern*

['The Festival Exhibition, 1951', *QEOM*, 57].
Map 10 (p. 132).

*Strand Palace Hotel, Strand, W.C.2*
Where Ron Bishop was staying.
['A Fine Beginning', *ST*, *CS*, 249].
Map 10 (p. 132).

*Swiss Tavern, 53 Old Compton Street, Soho, W.1*
Much frequented by Thomas.
[*CL*, 506: verse-letter to T. W. Earp (1 July 1943)].
Map 10 (p. 132).

*Thames*
(i) 'the riding Thames'.

['A Refusal to Mourn . . .', *PDJ*, 192].
(ii) (a) Into which lost visitors fell.
(b) Over which rainbows might arrive.
(c) The subject of a 3-D festival film.
(d) London's festive water-street.
['The Festival Exhibition, 1951', *QEOM*, 50, 55, 56-7].

*Tottenham, N.17*
(i) Young Thomas and Dan Jenkyn discuss whether Swansea F.C. will beat Tottenham Hotspur ('the Spurs').
['The Fight', *Portrait*, *CS*, 158].
(ii) The boy wears a cap in Tottenham Hotspur's colours and leaves it in the park.
['Patricia, Edith, and Arnold', *Portrait*, *CS*, 152].

*Wardour Street, Soho, W.1*
An area of pubs and clubs where Thomas was all too often to be found.
See also, *Horseshoe Club*, above.
[*CL*, 506: verse-letter to T. W. Earp (1 July 1943)].
Map 10 (p. 132).

*Waterloo Station, S.E.1*
The narrator recalls a boy pushing a pram full of firewood through a street near the station.
['The Crumbs of One Man's Year', *CS*, 314].

*West End*
(i) Where Samuel Bennet, Mr Allingham, and friends are going in the taxi.

['Four Lost Souls', *ST*, *CS*, 282].
(ii) (a) Where Mrs Mackenzie goes despite her poor health.
(b) Where a play runs for 15 years.
['The Londoner', *The Doctor and the Devils and Other Scripts*, 218, 226].
(iii) 'West End Negligée' is sold by Mog Edwards at Manchester House, Llaregyb.
[*UMW*, 49].
Map 10 (p. 132).

*Westminster Abbey, S.W.1*
Since 1 March 1982 Thomas has been commemorated in Poets' Corner by a floor panel of Penrhyn green slate engraved by the Welsh artist and sculptor, Jonah Jones. The panel reads
Dylan Thomas
27 October 1914
9 November 1953
Time held me green and dying
Though I sang in my chains like the sea.
Buried at Laugharne.

*2-6 West Street, W.C.2*
One of the addresses of Gryphon Films, Donald Taylor's successor to Strand Films. During the war Thomas wrote scripts for Gryphon.

*The Wheatsheaf, Rathbone Place, W.1*
In this pub, during April 1936, Thomas first met Caitlin Macnamara.
Map 10 (p. 132).

*Whitehall, S.W.1*
Where, Mr Allingham tells Samuel Bennet, there is a museum.

['A Fine Beginning', *ST*, *CS*, 251].


*Wimpole Street, W.1*
Thomas — a very young Thomas — cites
*The Barretts of Wimpole Street* as an example
of a successful play.
['The Sincerest Form of Flattery', *EP*, 93].
Map 10 (p. 132).

# CHAPTER SIX

# ENGLAND

# 'this... flat country'

Swansea Bay is a 'Devon-facing seashore' and even hazy Wales has many clear days. On each one, during his life in Swansea, young Dylan Thomas glimpsed Ilfracombe and the Devon coastline across the Bristol Channel. From his bedroom window and from Cwmdonkin Drive he could see England.

His life with Caitlin Macnamara found him often across the border: they, of course, were married in Penzance, honeymooned in Cornwall, and stayed often with Caitlin's mother in Ringwood, Hampshire. Then there were the periods spent in Beaconsfield, Bosham, Marshfield, Oxford and South Leigh. Llewellyn and Aeronwy were sent to English boarding schools.

But Thomas never felt wholly at home in English places. When living in them he didn't write very much of consequence. He grabbed at the chance to return to Laugharne in 1949. For the 'idea' of England was more compelling than, as it were, England itself. It was, for Thomas, the country where writers made their names because it included London and London beckoned all literary provincials. It is no accident that his English homes all had fairly easy access to the capital. His England may have been a 'flat country' in more ways than one, but his London was a constant and addictive 'high'.

REFERENCES TO ENGLAND

*Letter*
In Ringwood, Thomas waits for Llewellyn's birth, wishes he has money and is back in Laugharne: 'This flat English country levels the intelligence, planes down the imagination, narrows the a's'.
[*CL*: 352: to Charles Fisher (January 1939)].

*Works*
(i)   Complimentary remarks about the English film industry.
      ['The Films', *EP*, 88].

(ii) The poet asserts, rather improbably, that his world is, amongst other things, 'an English valley'.
['My World is Pyramid', *PDJ*, 105].

(iii)     'the horns of England
Summon your snowy horsemen'.
['Hold hard, these ancient minutes in the cuckoo's month', *PDJ*, 122].

(iv) Nant and the Narrator live far from the sea around England.
['The Lemon', *CS*, 58].

(v) The boy gazes at England over mountains and trees.
['A Prospect of the Sea', *CS*, 88, 90].

(vi) Thomas, the young reporter, writes his address as 'South Wales, England'. (This use, by a Welshman, of 'England' as, effectively, 'Britain', would be unlikely today; see *CL*, 636: to Mr & Mrs D. J. Thomas (5 June 1947), for another example.)
['Old Garbo', *Portrait*, *CS*, 210].

(vii) 'Man was the burning England she was sleep-walking', says Thomas of the poem's female subject.
['Into her lying down head', *PDJ*, 157].

(viii) (a) Most of Samuel Bennet's adventures take place in England.
(b) Part two begins in a room so over-furnished that it is 'the fullest room in England'.
['Plenty of Furniture', *ST*, *CS*, 262, and *ST*, *CS*, *passim*].

(ix) Beyond Wales, for Thomas when young, was 'England which was London'.
['Reminiscences of Childhood (Second Version)', *QEOM*, 9].

(x) (a) Where landladies' visitors buried themselves between holidays.
(b) Where the retired male nurse used to tend the rich and mad.
['Quite Early One Morning', *CS*, 291, 293].

(xi) In medieval England, says Raine satirically, there was *real* snow.
[*Rebecca's Daughters*, 24].

(xii) In England American slang is always ridiculously out-of-date, laments slang-collector Thomas.
['Idioms', *EP*, 162].

(xiii) Improbable though it may seem, some inhabitants of Laugharne may once have lived in England.
['Laugharne', *QEOM*, 70].

(xiv) (a) Where tall men with monocles may have been invented.
(b) Where some reactionaries say they fear going out alone at night.
['A Visit to America', *QEOM*, 64, 65].

*Ascot, Berkshire*
The famous race-course opens the children's alphabet-song.
[*Me and My Bike*, 39].

*Banbury, Oxfordshire*
(i)   The little girl sings 'Banbury Cross'.
      [*Me and My Bike*, 38].
(ii)  Thomas once confessed that he had been haunted by the 'Banbury Cross' nursery rhyme.
      ['Poetic Manifesto', *EP*, 155].

*Beaconsfield, Bucks.*
During 1944 the Thomases lived here with Donald Taylor, the film-producer.

*Birmingham, West Midlands*
(i)   In Paddington Station buffet was a 'cold, ordinary woman from Birmingham, driven off by a wink'.
      ['A Fine Beginning', *ST*, *CS*, 255].
(ii)  On a model of early Britain, Birmingham was an 'inferno of blown desert sand'.
      ['The Festival Exhibition, 1951', *QEOM*, 50].

*Bosham, Sussex*
In early 1944 the Thomases occupied a house named 'Far End'.
(i)   'very nice, too, looking over water'.
      [*CL*, 513: to T. W. Earp (prob. February 1944)].
(ii)  It was 'beastly', reported Thomas of their three months stay.
      [*CL*, 517 (27 July 1944)].

*Bristol, Avon*
(i)   Eleazer got the job with the waxworks partly because his rival from

Bristol had a harelip.
['Jarley's', *CS*, 349].
(ii)  A city, 'roaring with temptation', visited by Gwilym during a religious tour on which, he said, he met many actresses.
      ['The Peaches', *Portrait*, *CS*, 128].

*Buckinghamshire*
Where Cribbé, the rising writer, buys a cottage.
['How to be a Poet', *Prospect*, 110].

*Cambridge, Cambridgeshire*
Thomas read his poetry to the English Club on 7 December 1939.

*Cerne Abbas, Dorset*
Close to Ringwood (see below), where the Thomases often stayed, is the White Giant cut into the turf of Giant Hill. Almost certainly this is the source of the central symbol of Thomas's late poem, 'In the White Giant's Thigh'.

*Cheshire*
During April/May 1935 Thomas stayed with A.J.P. and Margaret Taylor in 'Three Gates' cottage, Higher Disley.

*Coventry, West England*
Visited by Thomas during 1944, when scripting 'Building the Future' for Gryphon Films.

*Devon*
See Chapter One / *Sands*.

*Dove, Cumbria*
In George Ring's quotation from Words-

worth.
['Four Lost Souls', *ST*, *CS*, 286].

*Dover Cliffs, Kent*
'whitefaced over the shifting sea-dyes'.
['Our Country', *QEOM (USA)*, 91].

*Epsom, Surrey*
'E for Epsom' is part of the children's
alphabet-song.
[*Me and My Bike*, 39].

*Eton, Berkshire*
*Letter:*
At nineteen Thomas resembles, he says, an
'emasculate Eton Boy'.
[*CL*, 37: to Pamela Hansford Johnson
(early November 1933)].
*Work:*
Eton's playing-fields were a place where
sense could be found.
['The first ten years in school and park',
*Notebooks*, 193].

*Gloucestershire*
Where Lady Quincey came from.
['The End of the River', *CS*, 50].

*Hampshire*
(i)    Full of 'slick-bonneted . . . road-
       houses'.
       [*CL*, 368: to Lawrence Durrell (prob.
       March 1939)].
(ii)   A 'flat, narrow-chested, and vowel-
       led county full of fading squires,
       traditional English romantic outlaws,
       sour gentlewomen and professional
       ostriches'.
       [*CL*, 364: to Bert Trick (March
       1939)].

*Horsham, Sussex*
At 10 North Street, Horsham, was Leslie
Andrews & Co., Thomas's accountants.

*Ilfracombe, Devon*
(i)    Where Ronald sailed from Swansea
       with a party from Brynhyfryd.
       ['One Warm Saturday', *Portrait*, *CS*,
       221].
(ii)   At which men looked from their
       deck-chairs on Swansea sands.
       ['Holiday Memory', *CS*, 308].

*Kingsley, Hampshire*
The home of Thomas's friend, T. W.
Earp.
['New Quay', *PDJ*, 179].

*Lancashire*
(i)    The lives of Lancashire cotton-
       weavers might provide material for a
       popular novel, suggests a cynical
       Thomas.
       ['How to begin a Story', *QEOM*, 39].
(ii)   The lives of Lancashire cotton-
       weavers *did* provide material for *The
       Warp*, *The Woof*, and *The Way*, the
       successful trilogy by Cribbe, the
       rising writer.
       ['How to be a Poet', *Prospect*, 109].

*Liverpool, Merseyside*
A place to which women intend — but
fail — to run away.
['A Fine Beginning', *ST*, *CS*, 248].

*Manchester, Greater Manchester*
At Llangollen, notes Thomas, 'Ukrainians
with Manchester accents gopak up the
hill'.

['The International Eisteddfod', *QEOM*, 59].

## Marshfield, Nr. Chippenham, Avon
Thomas's friend, John Davenport, lived at The Malting House, Marshfield. The Thomases stayed with him from July to September 1940. Here Thomas collaborated with Davenport in the writing of their satirical novel, *The Death of the King's Canary* (1940-1, but not published in full — due to allusions to contemporary literary figures — until 1976).

## Middlesex
Where Cribbe's volume of poetry, *Linnet and Spindle*, is noticed favourably.
['How to be a Poet', *Prospect*, 107].

## Mousehole, Cornwall
During the spring of 1936 Thomas stayed here with Wyn Henderson. In the following year she ran a guest-house called 'The Lobster Pot'. Thomas and Caitlin stayed in an adjoining cottage prior to their marriage on 11 July 1937 and for part of their honeymoon.
'the loveliest village in England'.
[*CL*, 222 (April 1936)].

## New Forest, Hampshire
When staying at Ringwood (below) Thomas and family often walked here. He writes scornfully of tweedy, sandalled writers from the New Forest area whom he saw in Salisbury pubs.
[*CL*, 377: to John Davenport (11 May 1939)].

*Mousehole (Lobster Pot)*

*Oxford — Holywell Ford Summer House*

## Newlyn, Cornwall
The Thomases stayed here, briefly, during July 1937, whilst on honeymoon. They occupied 'Fradgan Studios' owned by Max Chapman the painter.

## Ockham, Surrey
Where Thomas's friend T. W. Earp, the poet and art-critic, lived for a time. [CL, 520: verse-letter to T. W. Earp (1 September 1944)].

## Oxford, Oxfordshire
An important place for Thomas because of the patronage he received from Margaret Taylor, A. J. P. Taylor's first wife. Thomas's eldest child, Llewellyn, went to boarding-school in the city.

Where the poetry festival began before moving to London. ['The English Festival of Spoken Poetry', QEOM, 127].

### George Hotel
Now closed, this was a favourite Thomas pub near the railway station.

### Holywell Ford
From March 1946 to April 1947 the Thomases lived in a one-room summer-house in the garden of A.J.P & Margaret Taylor's home (behind Magdalen College off Cross Street).
(i) 'it is, I think, a converted telephone kiosk'.
    [CL, 587 (27 April 1946)].

*Penzance Registry Office*

(ii) 'here is feverish'.
[*CL*, 612: to Graham Greene (11 January 1947)].

*Magdalen College*
Where, Thomas writes, he has a room 'to read, write, dance & destroy poems in'.
[*CL*, 595: to Daniel Jones (24 June 1946)].

*Magdalen College School*
Llewellyn's private boarding-school.

*The Port Mahon, St Clement's*
A favourite Thomas pub.

## Penzance, Cornwall

### Lamorna Cove
Thomas and Caitlin Macnamara lived together at 'Oriental Cottage' during June 1937 shortly before their marriage.

### Porthcurno
Thomas stayed with Wyn Henderson at 'Polgigga', Porthcurno, Penzance, during April/May 1936. Describing himself as a true suburbanite he complained that the area was 'all scenery and landscape'.
[*CL*, 222 (April 1936)].

### Registry Office
Thomas married Caitlin Macnamara at Penzance Registry Office on 11 July 1937, 'with no money, no prospect of money, no attendant friends or relatives, and in complete happiness'.
[*CL*, 255 (15 July 1937)].

*Poole, Dorset*
Llewellyn Edouard, the Thomases' first child, was born in Cornelia Hospital on 30 January 1939. His parents had been staying at Ringwood.

*Ringwood, Hampshire*
Caitlin Macnamara's mother lived in New Inn House, Blashford, near Ringwood. The Thomases visited frequently and often sent Llewellyn to stay. They lived with Mrs Macnamara from late summer 1937 to spring 1938.
'a very lovely place'.
[*CL*, 261 (October 1937)].

> *The Royal Oak, Market Place*
> Where Dylan and Caitlin were regulars.

*St Ives, Cornwall*
A place to which women intend — but fail — to run away.
['A Fine Beginning', *ST, CS*, 248].

*Salisbury, Wilts.*
See *New Forest*, above.

*Shropshire*
Where eavesdropping in lady poets' torsoes was a favourite pastime.
['Spajma and Salnady', *EP*, 144].

*South Leigh, Oxfordshire*
The Thomases lived at 'The Manor House', a small cottage owned by Margaret Taylor, from August/September 1947 to April/May 1949.

A 'cowpad village'.
[*CL*, 692: to John Davenport (17 November 1948)].

> *The Masons Arms*
> The village pub where, inevitably, Dylan and Caitlin were regulars.

*Steyning, Sussex*
Victor Neuberg lived at Vine Cottage. As editor of 'Poets' Corner' in *The Sunday Referee*, he first brought Thomas's work to wide public notice.
(i)   Where the highbrow was exhibited.
      ['To Pamela Hansford Johnson', *EP*, 127].
(ii)  Where Spajma lay in a hammock.
      ['Spajma and Salnady', *EP*, 143].

*Sussex*
(i)   Stories should not be written about rural Sussex, 'where you can't hear the thrushes for the noise of typewriters'.
      ['How to begin a Story', *QEOM*, 41].
(ii)  A successful poet may have 'the look of all Sussex in his stingo'd eyes', and a car that drives itself there.
      ['How to be a Poet', *Prospect*, 105, 106].

*Tring Park, Hertfordshire*
Thomas's daughter, Aeronwy, was educated privately at the Arts Education School.

*Worcester, Hereford & Worcester*
Where a man, for a bet, ate fifty-two
pounds of plums.
['The Crumbs of One Man's Year', *CS*,
312].

*Yorkshire*
(a)  In which the story is set.
(b)  Fred, the boy, sings partly about the
     county.
(c)  Horses have Yorkshire accents.
(d)  Sir Gregory and Lady Grig think the
     Yorkshire ridings to be good places to
     ride.
     [*Me and My Bike*, 10, 11, 23].

# CHAPTER SEVEN

# NEW YORK

# 'nightmare city
...cosy as toast'

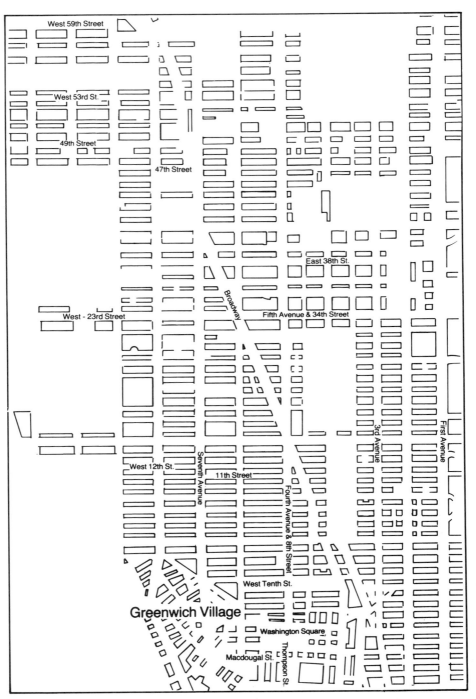

West 59th Street

West 53rd St.

49th Street

47th Street

Broadway

East 38th St.

West - 23rd Street

Fifth Avenue & 34th Street

3rd Avenue

First Avenue

West 12th St.

Seventh Avenue

11th Street

Fourth Avenue & 8th Street

West Tenth St.

Greenwich Village

Washington Square

Macdougal St.

Thompson St.

*New York*

New York was Dylan Thomas's first sight of the U.S.A. On 21 February 1950 he landed at Idlewild (now Kennedy) airport for his first visit, to be met by John Malcolm Brinnin, acting as his American agent, who almost immediately took him on a tour of the city's bars and sights. Three months later, after the wildly-successful reading-tour, he sailed home from New York on the *Queen Elizabeth*. For his second visit he and Caitlin arrived by sea, on the *Queen Mary*, and left in the same way, on the Dutch liner, the *Niew Amsterdam*. Visit 3 saw him again sailing in, on the *S.S. United States*, and flying home from Idlewild. He flew in for his final visit and the *S.S. United States* took his body home.

Throughout his life Thomas had, unwittingly, prepared himself for this encounter with the new world at its most extreme: he had been weaned on Hollywood films and remained a fan of gangster stories. Nevertheless, New York at first overwhelmed him until he found his own city, a more homely place, by New York standards, in the Chelsea and Greenwich Village areas. During each visit to the U.S.A. this part of New York became his base, for there, more than anywhere else in that country, he felt at home.

In New York Thomas was lionised, made friends, behaved badly, had some of his most brilliant public successes, and died.

REFERENCES TO NEW YORK

*Letters*

(i)    On his first visit Thomas writes dutifully to his parents, putting a respectable gloss on his activities but conveying vividly his first impressions of 'this titanic dream world, soaring Babylon . . . this mad city . . . the nightmare city'.
       [*CL*, 750: to Mr & Mrs D. J. Thomas (26 February 1950)].
(ii)   From Laugharne, to an American acquaintance, himself a poet, who helped him place poems in American magazines, Thomas recalls the city of that first visit as 'pretty New York'.
       [*CL*, 798: to Oscar Williams (28 May 1951)].

# Work

'after the ulcerous rigours of a lecturer's spring, New York is a haven cosy as toast, cool as an icebox, and safe as skyscrapers'.
['A Visit to America', *QEOM*, 69. See also, 63-4. 66-7].

*Barnard College, Broadway & West*
*116th Street*
Reading:
Visit 1 — Thursday, 18 May 1950.

*Beekman Tower Hotel*

*Beekman Tower Hotel, First Avenue &*
*49th Street*
Where Thomas first stayed in New York. He was soon asked to leave.
Map 11 (p. 164).

*Brooklyn*
Associated with gangster stories.
['How to begin a Story', *QEOM*, 38].
Map 11 (p. 164).

*Chelsea Hotel, Seventh Avenue & West*
*23rd Street*
Where, for Visit 2, Dylan and Caitlin rented a small apartment. Thomas himself stayed here during Visits 3 and 4. On 5 November 1953 he was taken, in a coma, from his Chelsea apartment to St Vincent's R.C. Hospital (see below) and did not return.
'Chelsea'd New York'.
[*CL*, 880: to John Malcolm Brinnin (18 March 1953)].
Map 11 (p. 164).

*Cherry Lane Theatre,*
*38 Commerce Street*
Reading:
Visit 2 — Sunday, 24 February 1952.

*Cinema 16, Irving Place*
On Wednesday, 28 October 1953 — only

*Chelsea Hotel*

a few days before he collapsed and died —
Thomas took part, with Arthur Miller and
others, in a symposium on 'Poetry and the
Film' arranged by a group of New York
intellectuals known as 'Cinema 16'. Miller
recalls the venue as 'a high school auditorium in the Irving Place area'.

*Circle-in-the-Square Theatre,*
*1633 Broadway*
Reading:
Visit 2 — Sunday, 16 March 1952.
Map 11 (p. 164).

*City College of New York, Convent*
*Avenue & 139th Street*
Reading:
Visit 4 — Thursday, 29 October 1953.
This was Thomas's last public reading.

*Columbia University, Broadway & West*
*116th Street*
Reading:
Visit 1 — Monday, 13 March 1950.

Cooper Union, Fourth Avenue &
8th Street
Reading:
Visit 1 — Monday, 24 April 1950.
Map 11 (p. 164).

East River
Where Thomas heard ships hooting in the
night.
[CL, 750: to Mr & Mrs D. J. Thomas (26
February 1950)].
Map 11 (p. 164).

East Side
Part of Brinnin's guided tour for the
newly-arrived Thomas.
'where the Dead End Kids come from'.
[CL, 750: to Mr & Mrs D. J. Thomas (26
February 1950)].

Empire State Building, Fifth Avenue &
34th Street
From the top of which Thomas was glad
to return.
[CL, 750: to Mr & Mrs D. J. Thomas (26
February 1950)].
Map 11 (p. 164).

Gotham Book Mart, 41 West
47th Street
Where parties were given for Thomas
during Visit 1.
Map 11 (p. 164).

Grand Ticino Restaurant,
Thompson Street
The Italian restaurant in Greenwich
Village where Brinnin took Thomas on 21
February 1950, his first day in the U.S.A.
Map 11 (p. 164).

Greenwich Village
Thomas's favourite American place. He
drank frequently in village bars. During
Visit 3 he loved to walk through the
Village with his mistress, Liz Reitell.
Map 11 (p. 164).

Harlem
  'the black, the yellow and mulatto
From Harlem'.
['We who are young are old', PDJ, 41;
Notebooks, 170].

Hotel Earle, Waverly Place, Washington
Square N.W.
Where Thomas stayed during Visit 1, in
April 1950.
Map 11 (p. 164).

Julius's Bar, West 10th Street &
Waverley Place
During Visit 1 Thomas drank here with
Brinnin.
Map 11 (p. 164).

Master Institute of United Arts,
310 Riverside Drive
This Institute, long defunct, is referred to
by writers on Thomas (almost certainly
incorrectly) as the 'Masters Institute'. The
building is now an apartment house.
Reading:
Visit 2 — Wednesday, 30 April 1952.

Midston House, 22 East 38th Street
Where Thomas stayed during Visit 1,
after having to leave the Beekman Tower
Hotel.
Map 11 (p. 164).

*Hotel Earle*

*Minetta Tavern, 113 Macdougal Street*
A favourite — and surviving — bar of
Thomas's in Greenwich Village.
Map 11 (p. 164).

*Museum of Modern Art, 11 West
53rd Street*
Readings:
Visit 1 — Monday, 24 April 1950.
Visit 2 — Tuesday, 5 February 1952.
            Monday, 18 February 1952.
Map 11 (p. 164).

*New School for Social Research, 66 West
12th Street*

Readings:
Visit 2 — Wednesday, 13 February 1952
            Wednesday, 12 March 1952.
Map 11 (p. 164).

*New York University,
Washington Square*
Readings:
Visit 2 — Thursday, 14 February 1952.
            Thursday, 31 February 1952.
Map 11 (p. 164).

*St Luke's Episcopal Chapel of Trinity
Parish, 487 Hudson Street*
Where a memorial service for Thomas

*St Vincent's Hospital*

was held during November 1953.
Map 11 (p. 164).

### St Vincent's Roman Catholic Hospital, Seventh Avenue & 11th Street

Thomas was admitted in a coma at 1.58 a.m. on Thursday, 5 November 1953. He never regained consciousness and died at about midday on Monday, 9 November 1953. The post-mortem report recorded, in effect, that he died of drink.
Map 11 (p. 164).

### Socialist Party in New York City, 303 Fourth Avenue

Reading:
Visit 2 — Friday, 29 February 1952.
Map 11 (p. 164).

### Steinway Hall, 111 West 57th Street

On Friday, 22 February 1952 (Visit 2) Thomas here made the first recordings of his works: five poems (including 'Fern Hill' and 'Do not go gentle') and 'A Child's Christmas in Wales', for Barbara Holdridge and Marianne Mantell, who had recently formed Caedmon Records. During Visit 3 — on 2 June 1953 — he returned to the Steinway to make further recordings for them.

The hall has since been incorporated into the Manhattan Life Insurance Company building.
Map 11 (p. 164).

### Third Avenue

In Thomas's time this was an area of Irish saloon bars. He was a regular visitor from

*Third Avenue*

*White Horse Tavern – Sign over entrance*

his first day in the U.S.A.
Map 11 (p. 164).

*Washington Square*
Admired by Thomas. During Visit 1 he
stayed for a time at the nearby Hotel Earle
(see above).
Map 11 (p. 164).

*White Horse Tavern, Hudson Street*
Thomas's favourite New York bar. He
drank there regularly on each American
visit; it is said he was there on the night of
his final collapse. A picture of him now
hangs in the bar-room.
Map 11 (p. 164).

*Young Men's and Young Women's
Hebrew Association Poetry Center,*

*White Horse Tavern – Mirror behind bar*

172

YM & YWHA

*Kaufmann Auditorium, Lexington Avenue & East 92nd Street.*
John Malcolm Brinnin, as Director of the YH & YWHA's Poetry Center, arranged Thomas's American tours. Each had, as its centre-piece, a number of brilliantly successful readings in the Kaufman Auditorium.
Readings:
Visit 1 — Thursday, 23 February 1950.
Saturday, 25 February 1950.
Monday, 15 May 1950.
Visit 2 — Thursday, 31 January 1952.
Saturday, 2 February 1952.
Thursday, 15 May 1952.
Visit 3 — Friday, 8 May 1953

Thursday, 14 May 1953 — the première of *Under Milk Wood* recorded by Caedmon Records.
Sunday, 24 May 1953.
Thursday, 28 May 1953 — the second performance of *Under Milk Wood.*
Visit 4 — Saturday, 24 October 1953 — the third performance of *Under Milk Wood.*
Sunday, 25 October 1953 — Thomas's last performance of *Under Milk Wood.*

# CHAPTER EIGHT

# U.S.A.

## 'the gravy pots'

Dylan Thomas's work was first published in the U.S.A. in 1939: *The World I Breathe*, a selection of poetry and prose, was brought out by James Laughlin IV, who had recently founded *New Directions*. His company has remained Thomas's American publisher.

When World War Two ended a penniless Thomas began to sound American acquaintances about the possibility of lucrative visits to read, or to lecture, or perhaps to take up a university post. The first firm invitation arrived in 1949 from John Malcolm Brinnin, the new Director of the Young Men's and Young Women's Hebrew Association Poetry Center in New York City. Brinnin arranged readings at the Center and throughout the country; under his auspices Thomas made four visits:

Visit 1: 21 February 1950 to 31 May 1950.
Visit 2: 20 January 1952 to 16 May 1952 (with Caitlin).
Visit 3: 21 April 1953 to 3 June 1953.
Visit 4: 19 October 1953 to 9 November 1953.

Visit 4 ended with Thomas's death. His body was shipped back to Wales for burial at Laugharne on 24 November 1953.

The four visits enhanced and consolidated Thomas's international reputation, not least by making him a famous public-reader and recording him in action. And, as everyone knows, he became an international byword for scandalous behaviour. The U.S.A. was the setting for the most destructive part of his almost-eager pilgrimage to that small hotel room in New York and alcohol's lethal coma.

For a humorous general account of lecturing in the U.S.A. see 'A Visit to America', *QEOM*, 63-9.

176

REFERENCES TO THE U.S.A.

## Letters

(i) In a letter from New Quay a desperately hard-up Thomas sounds his American poet acquaintance about transatlantic prospects: 'I'd love a little ladleful from the gravy pots over there — a lick of the ladle, the immersion of a single hair in the rich shitbrown cauldron'.
[*CL*, 550: to Oscar Williams (28 March 1945)].

(ii) Thomas tells his publisher of Brinnin's invitation, and confesses to nervousness: America 'puts the fear of Mammon in me'.
[*CL*, 722: to James Laughlin IV (13 October 1949)].

(iii) For 'Princess Caetani', see Chapter Three, Letter ix. His second visit to America is one of Thomas's excuses for not completing *Under Milk Wood*: 'I buried my head in the sands of America: flew over America like a damp, ranting bird; boomed and fiddled while home was burning'.
[*CL*, 844: to Marguerite Caetani (6 November 1952)].

(iv) As Thomas prepares for his third visit, without Caitlin, he reveals, semi-facetiously, growing domestic tensions. In the U.S.A. he found, as he puts it, 'appreciation, dramatic work, and friends', which, for Caitlin, means 'flattery, idleness, and infidelity'.
[*CL*, 879: to John Malcolm Brinnin (18 March 1953)].

## Works

(i) A discussion of American films.
['The Films', *EP*, 88].

(ii) Where Appreciation Hours are to be found.
['The first ten years in school and park', *Notebooks*, 194].

(iii) Young Thomas, on his way to camp, imagines he is heading for 'Rhossilli, U.S.A.'.
['Extraordinary Little Cough', *Portrait*, *CS*, 166].

(iv) Young reporter Thomas sees a romantic film about American college life.
['Old Garbo', *Portrait*, *CS*, 210-11].

(v) The small boy wishes that an imaginary uncle might arrive from America 'with revolvers and St Bernards'.
['Patricia, Edith, and Arnold', *Portrait*, *CS*, 145].

(vi) Where Mr Theodore Bear died.
['Memories of Christmas', *QEOM*, 22].

(vii) If a bad but rich poet is in America then he can be attacked, a cynical Thomas advises would-be reviewers.

['How to be a Poet', *Prospect*, 113].

(viii) The fascination of American slang.
['Idioms', *EP*, 162].

(ix) An innocent lecturer from Britain — as Thomas himself was, once — can be seen, American-bound, 'going buoyantly west to his remunerative doom'. ['A Visit to America', *QEOM*, 67. See also, 63-69].

*Amherst*

*Amherst, Mass.*
Where, according to Thomas, he made his audiences suffer.
[*CL*, 894: to Theodore Roethke (19 June 1953)].
Readings:
Visit 1 — Friday, 3 March 1950 — Amherst College.
Visit 3 — Wednesday, 20 May 1953 — Amherst College.


*Ann Arbor, Michigan*
Reading:
Visit 1 — Wednesday, 3 May 1950 —

University of Michigan.


*Annandale-on-Hudson, N.Y.*
Reading:
Visit 2 — Thursday, 8 May 1952 — Bard College.


*Baltimore, Maryland*
Reading:
Visit 2 — Tuesday, 4 March 1952 — Johns Hopkins University.

*University of California, Berkeley*

179

*Bennington, Vermont*
Where, Thomas recalled mysteriously, he had felt 'curiously thwarted'.
[*CL*, 894: to Theodore Roethke (19 June 1953)].
Reading:
Visit 3 — Monday, 27 April 1953 — Bennington College.


*Berkeley, Cal.*
Readings:
Visit 1 — Tuesday, 4 April 1950 — University of California.
Visit 2 — Tuesday, 15 April 1952 — University of California.


*Big Sur, Cal.*
During Visit 2 the Thomases journeyed to Big Sur to meet Henry Miller.


*Bloomington, Indiana*
Readings:
Visit 1 —   Friday, 5 May 1950 — Indiana University.
Friday, 5 May 1950 — Indiana University (lecture on Thomas's work in documentary films).


*Boston, Mass.*
Where an audience could be 'a bunch of dead pans and wealthy pots'.
['A Visit to America', *QEOM*, 67].
Readings:
Visit 2 — Tuesday, 11 March 1952 — Boston University.

Visit 3 — Saturday, 25 April 1953 — Boston University.


*Boston Harbour, Mass.*
Of which the Fat Man shows Annie a picture.
['After the Fair', *CS*, 3].


*Bronxville, N.Y.*
Reading:
Visit 2 — Monday, 12 May 1952 — Sarah Lawrence College.


*Bryn Mawr, Pennsylvania*
Reading:
Visit 1 — Tuesday, 7 March 1950 — Bryn Mawr College.


*Burlington, Vermont*
Reading:
Visit 2 — Friday, 15 February 1952 — University of Vermont.


*California*
Part of the tour made by European lecturers.
['A Visit to America', *QEOM*, 63].


*Cambridge, Mass.*
During Visit 3 Thomas wrote part of *Under Milk Wood* when staying with Brinnin at 100 Memorial Drive.
Readings:

*Boston University*

Visit 1 — Wednesday, 1 March 1950 — Harvard University.
Thursday, 2 March 1950 — Thomas recorded his poetry for the Sweeney Collection in the Lamont Library, Harvard University.

Visit 2 — Friday, 7 March 1952 — Massachussetts Institute of Technology.
Monday, 10 March 1952 — at the Brattle Theatre for The Poets' Theatre.

Visit 3 — Friday, 1 May 1953 — at the Fogg Museum, Harvard University, for The Poets' Theatre.
Sunday, 3 May 1953 — at the Fogg Museum, Harvard University. A solo performance, for The Poets' Theatre, of the unfinished *Under Milk Wood.*
Monday, 11 May 1953 — Massachussetts Institute of Technology.

*Chicago*

*Chicago, Illinois*
One of Thomas's favourite American cities. He drank in South Side bars with the novelist Nelson Algren.
Readings:
Visit 1 — Thursday, 16 March 1950 — University of Chicago.
Visit 2 — Wednesday, 23 April 1952 — for *Poetry Magazine*.

*Letters:*
(i) Included in Thomas's list of things and places that frightened him.
[*CL*, 766: to Mr & Mrs John Nimms (17 July 1950)].
(ii) The only place in the mid-West that Thomas wished to revisit.
[*CL*, 796: to John Malcolm Brinnin (12 April 1951)].

*Work:*
A place associated with gangster stories. ['How to begin a Story', *QEOM*, 38].

*Claremont, Cal.*
Reading:
Visit 1 — Tuesday, 11 April 1950 — Pomona College.

*Columbia, Missouri*
Reading:
Visit 2 — Monday, 21 April 1952 — University of Missouri.

*Detroit, Michigan*
Reading:
Visit 1 — Thursday, 4 May 1950 — Wayne State University.


*Durham, North Carolina*
Reading:
Visit 3 — Tuesday, 12 May 1953 — Duke University.


*Evanston, Illinois*
Reading:
Visit 2 — Thursday, 24 April 1952 — Northwestern University.


*Flagstaff, Arizona*
During Visit 2 the Thomases stayed here with the Max Ernsts and sent home a mock obituary.
[*CL*, 825: to Daniel Jones (21 March 1952)].


*Gainsville, Florida*
Reading:
Visit 1 — Thursday, 27 April 1950 — at Florida Union Auditorium, for the Creative Writing Collection of the University of Florida Library.


*Gambier, Ohio*
Reading:
Visit 1 — Wednesday, 15 March 1950 — Kenyon College.


*Geneva, N.Y.*
Reading:
Visit 1 — Wednesday, 26 April 1950 — Hobart College.


*Hanover, New Hampshire*
Reading:
Visit 2 — Tuesday, 13 May 1952 — Dartmouth College.


*Hollywood, Cal.*
Visited during Visit 1, when Christopher Isherwood was one of his hosts. Thomas met Shelley Winters and Chaplin, spending an evening at the latter's home.
'shining Hollywood'.
['Into her lying down head', *LVW*, 93; not in *PDJ* version].


*Iowa City, Iowa*
Thomas stayed here for almost two weeks (March/April 1950) during Visit 1, one of his hosts being the poet Robert Lowell.
Reading:
Visit 1 — Tuesday, 21 March 1950 — State University of Iowa.


*Ithaca, N.Y.*
Reading:
Visit 1 — Tuesday, 14 March 1950 — Cornell University.


*Kansas City, Kansas*
Where Hugo de Hugo was born.
['The Sincerest Form of Flattery', *EP*, 91].

*Iowa State University*

*Lincoln, Mass.*
Reading:
Visit 2 — Friday, 7 March 1952 — De Cordova Museum.

*Lynchburg, Virginia*
Reading:
Visit 3 — Tuesday, 5 May 1953 — Smith Memorial Auditorium, Randolph-Macon Women's College, for the Public Lecture Committee and the Department of English at Randolph-Macon.

*Los Angeles, Cal.*
A venue for all kinds of European lecturers.
['A Visit to America', *QEOM*, 64].
Reading:
Visit 1 — Monday, 10 April 1950 — University of California at Los Angeles.

*Millbrook, N.Y.*
Home of the photographer Rollie McKenna. The Thomases stayed with her during Visit 2.
Reading:
Visit 2 — Tuesday, 26 February 1952 —

Bennett Junior College.

*Milwaukee, Wisconsin*
Reading:
Visit 2 — Friday, 25 April 1952 — Marquette University.

*Nantucket, Mass.*
'I lost my step in Nantucket', says First Drowned.
[*UMW*, 3].

*New Haven, Connecticut*
Reading:
Visit 1 — Tuesday, 28 February 1950 — Yale University.

*New Orleans, Louisiana*
Reading (scheduled):
Visit 2 — Monday, 28 April 1952 — Tulane University. This reading was the only one that Thomas ever cancelled.

*Norfolk, Connecticut*
Where Thomas's American publishers, James Laughlin IV's *New Directions*, was then located.

*Notre Dame, Indiana*
Reading:
Visit 1 — Friday, 17 March 1950 — Notre Dame University.

*Oakland, Cal.*
Reading:
Visit 1 — Monday, 17 April 1950 — Mills College.

*Philadelphia, Pennsylvania*
Reading:
Visit 3 — prob. Saturday, 9 May 1952 — Ethical Culture Society Auditorium, Ritenhouse Square, for the Philadelphia Art Alliance.

*Pittsburgh, Pennsylvania*
Thomas was invited to attend an international literary conference here in October 1953 (during his final Visit). He never made it.

*Poughkeepsie, N.Y.*
Reading:
Visit 1 — Tuesday, 9 May 1950 — Vassar College.

*Princeton, New Jersey*
Readings:
Visit 1 — Wednesday, 10 May 1950 — Princeton University.
Visit 2 — Wednesday, 5 March 1952 — Princeton University.

*Salt Lake City, Utah*
See *Utah*, below.

*San Francisco, Cal.*
A favourite place of the touring Thomas.
(i) Where visitors to the Festival of

*San Francisco State University, Anderson Hall*

Britain had, they said, seen better shows.
['The Festival Exhibition, 1951', *QEOM*, 52].

(ii) 'Between Frisco and Wales
 You were my bosun'
says Rosie Probert to Captain Cat.
[*UMW*, 69].

*San Francisco Museum of Art*
Reading:
Visit 2 — Wednesday, 16 April 1952.

*San Francisco State College*
Readings:
Visit 1 — Tuesday, 18 April 1950.
Visit 2 — Thursday, 3 April 1952.

*1520 Willard Street*
Home of Ruth Witt-Diamant, who ran the San Francisco State College Poetry Center and organised Thomas's readings. Thomas stayed here during Visit 1 and again, with Caitlin, during Visit 2.

*Santa Barbara, Cal.*
Reading:
Visit 1 — Thursday, 13 April 1950 — for Santa Barbara Museum and Santa Barbara College.

*Saratoga Springs, N.Y.*
Reading:
Visit 2 — Thursday, 13 March 1952 — Skidmore College.

*Seattle, Washington State*
The University of Washington has sad links with Swansea. Long after Thomas's death — in 1967 — his close friend Vernon Watkins died here suddenly when Visiting Professor of Poetry.

*Washington State University, Seattle*

Readings:
Visit 1 — Friday, 7 April 1950 — University of Washington.
Visit 2 — Thursday, 10 April 1952 — University of Washington.

*South Hadley, Mass.*
Reading:
Visit 1 — Thursday, 2 March 1950 — Mount Holyoke College.

*Storrs, Connecticut*
Readings:

Visit 2 — Wednesday, 7 May 1952 — University of Connecticut.
Visit 3 — Wednesday, 13 May 1953 — University of Connecticut.

*Syracuse, N.Y.*
Reading:
Visit 3 — Tuesday, 28 April 1953 — Syracuse University.

*Texas*
A desperately penniless Thomas was pre-

pared, he said, to live 'even in a kennel, Texas', if a wealthy patron could be found there. He never went to Texas.
[*CL*, 559: to Oscar Williams (30 July 1945)].


*University Park, Pennsylvania*
Visit 2 — Monday, 17 March 1952 — Pennsylvania State University.


*Urbana, Illinois*
Reading:
Visit 1 — Monday, 20 March 1950 — University of Illinois.


*Utah*

    *Salt Lake City*
    Reading:
    Visit 2 — Friday, 18 April 1952 — University of Utah. Thomas commemorated his visit in the characters of Mr and Mrs Utah Watkins of Salt Lake Farm.
    [*UMW*, 17, 19, 75, 76].


*Waltham, Mass.*
Reading:
Visit 1 — Tuesday, 2 May 1950 — Brandeis University.


*Washington D.C.*
Readings:
Visit 1 —   Wednesday, 8 March 1950 — Institute of Contemporary Arts — the reading

was sponsored by Robert Richman.
          Thursday, 9 March 1950 — Thomas recorded his work at the Library of Congress.
Visit 2 —  Friday, 8 February 1952 — I.C.A.
          Saturday, 1 March 1952 — I.C.A.
          (prob.) Monday, 5 May 1952 — I.C.A.
          Wednesday, 14 May 1952 — Duncan Phillips Gallery.
Visit 3 —  Monday, 4 May 1953 — I.C.A.


*Wellesley, Mass.*
Reading:
Visit 1 — Monday, 1 May 1950 — Wellesley College.


*Westport, Connecticut*
During Visit 1 John Malcolm Brinnin lived at Valley Road, Westport. Thomas stayed with him in February 1950.


*Williamstown, Mass.*
Reading:
Visit 3 — Wednesday, 29 April 1953 — Williams College.

CHAPTER NINE

# OTHER PLACES

# 'Abyssinia to Zanzibar'

Thomas's other places are varied, far-flung, and sometimes exotic. They include Italy, where Dylan and family sweated through the hot summer of 1947. They include Bahrein and Iran, visited for abortive film-making, Montreal and Vancouver, which were on his American reading-circuits, Eire, a persisting connection, and Scotland, where he went only once.

The imagination explored other areas. His childhood's Sunday Schools led him to Biblical towns and holy places; ships steamed from Swansea docks to remote destinations that glowed in Thomas's mind: the Antipodes, China, India. Out of the early reading and the period's popular mythology came stereotypes: a Canada of trappers, geisha'd Japan, snowy Lapland, naughty Paris, a luxurious Riviera. And the poet in him seized upon strangeness — Africa, Arabia, Egypt — and savoured the seductive sounds of Abyssinia, Asia, Madagascar, Zanzibar.

All such locations are diversions from familiar obsessions. Only a few places — known or imagined — were capable, through their sustained presence, of inspiring Thomas's finest literary achievements.

ABYSSINIA

Nineteen-thirties' slang: 'Abyssinia (I'll be seeing you)!' says the narrator to Tom and Walter.
['Just Like Little Dogs', *Portrait*, *CS*, 180].

AFRICA

(i) Discussed by the boys in the park.
['Reminiscences of Childhood (Second Version)', *QEOM*, 9].
(ii) Where the travelling horse neighed.
['The Horse's Ha', *CS*, 60].

*Sahara*
'Sahara in a shell'.
['Ballad of the Long-Legged Bait', *PDJ*, 165].

ALPS

See *SWITZERLAND* below.

ANTARCTICA

Where the rocking wind came from.
['The Orchards', *CS*, 42].

ANTIPODES

(i) The name of the speaker.
['Altarwise by owl-light — III', *PDJ*, 118].
(ii) Connected to Swansea by the sea.
['Holiday Memory', *CS*, 307].

## ARABIA
To which the child wished to ride his rocking-horse.
['The Tree', CS, 6].

### Arabian Sea
Hassan and the narrator sailed across.
['Hassan's Journey into the World', Notebooks, 82].

## ARCTIC
Scurries of Arctic snow fall on the poet's grave.
['My World is Pyramid', PDJ, 105].

### Kara Sea
A cold woman wailed nearby.
['The Orchards', CS, 42].

## ASIA
(i)   'straws' from Asia are in the poet's mouth.
      ['My World is Pyramid', PDJ, 105].
(ii)  'A climbing sea from Asia had me down'.
      ['Altarwise by owl-light — V', PDJ, 118].
(iii) The Devil, disguised as a snake, had 'The central plains of Asia in his garden'.
      ['Incarnate Devil', PDJ, 121; Notebooks, 311].
(iv)  It covers the garden of Eden.
      ['A Prospect of the Sea', CS, 91].
(v)   We dream, says the sorcerer, of naked Asian queens.
      ['Prologue to an Adventure', CS, 106].

## ATLANTIC
(i)   The poet turns through 'the Atlantic corn'.
      ['My World is Pyramid', PDJ, 105].
(ii)  'the Atlantic thighs
      Of Mrs Rosser Tea and Little Nell the Knock'.
      ['A Pub Poem', PDJ, 242].
(iii) A bad novel can sell well on both sides.
      ['A Visit to America', QEOM, 65].

### Biscay
A place of amorous bulls and calves.
['Ballad of the Long-Legged Bait', PDJ, 164].

## AUSTRALASIA
Birthplace of Hugo de Hugo's father.
['The Sincerest Form of Flattery', EP, 91].

## AUSTRALIA
Where Lady Quincey had a cousin.
['The End of the River', CS, 50].

## AUSTRIA
(i)   Where the poet imagines himself shot.
      ['My World is Pyramid', PDJ, 105].
(ii)  A country of songs about mowers on mountains.
      ['The International Eisteddfod', QEOM, 61].

## BAHREIN
Visited by Thomas in 1951 when he worked in the Gulf on a film-script for the Anglo-Iranian Oil Company.
      See IRAN below.

## BISCAY
See ATLANTIC, above.

*Vancouver, Canada*

## BRITAIN

The history of which was explained and celebrated by the Festival of Britain.
['The Festival Exhibition, 1951', *QEOM*, 52].

## BULGARIA

Salnady wishes to see a Bulgarian spy eating spinach.
['Spajma and Salnady', *EP*, 145].

## CANADA

*Hudson Bay*
Located near a wintry Mumbles Road, Swansea, think young Thomas and friend Jim.
['A Child's Christmas in Wales', *CS*, 296].

*Montreal*
Reading:
Visit 2 — Thursday, 28 February 1952 — McGill University.

*Niagara*
(i)   The grass is greener than 'Niagara's devil'.
['The Holy Six', *CS*, 101].
(ii)  Lord Cut-Glass has 'Niagara clocks that cataract their ticks'.
[*UMW*, 65].

*Vancouver*
Readings:
Visit 1 — Thursday, 6 April 1950 — University of British Columbia.
Visit 2 — Tuesday, 8 April 1952 — University of British Columbia.
— Wednesday, 9 April 1952 — reading arranged by a local sponsor.

*Yukon*
Where a trapper had false teeth.
['Spajma and Salnady', *EP*, 145].

## CEYLON

Where Basil's Colonel got the special recipe.
['How to be a Poet', *Prospect*, 112].

## CHINA

(i)    Part of the world for which the young Narrator feels conflicting emotions.
['Just Like Little Dogs', *Portrait*, *CS*, 177].
(ii)   The small boy's garden walls seem like Great Walls.
['Patricia, Edith, and Arnold', *Portrait*, *CS*, 144].
(iii)  A magical destination for ships from Swansea docks.
['Reminiscences of Childhood (Second Version)', *QEOM*, 8].

## CZECHOSLOVAKIA

*Prague*
Visited by Thomas as a guest of the Czech government to attend the inauguration of the Czech Writers' Union. He stayed for almost a week from 4 March 1949.
   'Student of Prague' is one of Salnady's favourite films.
['Spajma and Salnady', *EP*, 142].

## DENMARK

*Copenhagen*
Thought, by Festival of Britain visitors, to have better shows.
['The Festival Exhibition, 1951', *QEOM*, 52].

## EGYPT

(i)    The poem's setting.

['Osiris, Come to Isis', *Notebooks*, 47-50].

(ii) The country that provides the poet with armour.
['My World is Pyramid', *PDJ*, 104].

(iii) Where bearded 'time' can be found and, it seems, mummies exhumed.
['Should lanterns shine', *PDJ*, 116].

(iv) One of 'time's' places.
['The Mouse and the Woman', *CS*, 84].

(v) Where, says the girl, she has a sister.
['A Prospect of the Sea', *CS*, 90].

*Cairo*
'dead Cairo's henna'.
['Altarwise by owl-light — IX', *PDJ*, 120].

*Nile*
(i) The main subject of the poem.
['Osiris, Come to Isis', *Notebooks*, 47-50].

(ii) With which a crocodile is associated.
['I, in my intricate image', *PDJ*, 111].

# EIRE

Ireland, whether Northern Ireland or Eire, was, to Thomas, simply 'Ireland'. He first stayed in the south in 1935, aged 21, and visited again in the 1940s, this time with Caitlin and friends. Caitlin, of course, was Irish through and through. Thomas scripted O'Sullivan's story, *Twenty Years A'Growing*, and admired Yeats and Joyce, so that, throughout his life, 'Ireland' was a persisting presence. See *NORTHERN IRELAND,* below.
*Letters:*
(i) 'this lazy and vocal land'.
[*CL*, 191-2: to Bert Trick (Summer 1935)].

(ii) 'Ireland was lovely'.
[*CL*, 599 (26 August 1946)].

*Works*
(i) The Fat Man from Treorchy describes Irish summers.
['After the Fair', *CS*, 3].

(ii) The fluent and sentimental Mr O'Brien is Lou's 'sugar daddy from old Ireland'.
['One Warm Saturday', *Portrait, CS,* 230].

(iii) Young Thomas imagines the Worm's Head at Rhossilli sailing across to Ireland; the young men would meet Yeats and kiss the Blarney Stone.
['Who Do You Wish Was With Us?', *Portrait, CS,* 201].

(iv) In Ireland live lovers of music-making.
['The International Eisteddfod', *QEOM*, 60].

*Aran Islands, County Galway*
'like a tree on Aran'.
['I, in my intricate image', *PDJ*, 111].

*Ardara, County Donegal*
*Letter:*
'a village you can't be too far from'.
[*CL*, 190: to Bert Trick (Summer 1935].
*Work:*
Birthplace of Fallon and Mrs Flynn.
[*The Doctor and the Devils*, Section 90, p. 92].

*Blarney, County Cork*
To kiss the stone would be one reason for sailing across to Ireland on Rhossilli's Worm's Head.
['Who Do You Wish Was With Us?', *Portrait, CS,* 201].

*Blasket Islands, County Kerry*
The setting of most of Thomas's film-script (1944) of Maurice O'Sullivan's story, *Twenty Years A'Growing*.

*County Clare*
Where Caitlin's family, the Macnamaras, originated.

*Dingle, County Kerry*
The setting of the opening of Thomas's film-script of *Twenty Years A'Growing*.

*County Donegal*
(a) A part of Eire where, Fallon implies, people are sometimes noisily drunk.
(b) Mrs Flynn says she comes from Donegal, following her son.
[*The Doctor and the Devils*, Section 90, pp. 91, 92; Section 99, p. 102; Section 101, p. 103].

*Dublin*
Visited by Dylan and Caitlin during August 1946, when on holiday with Bill and Helen McAlpine.

*Galway, County Galway*
'G for Galway Races', sing the children.
[*Me and My Bike*, 39].

*Glen Lough, County Donegal*
Thomas stayed here, in a farm cottage, with Geoffrey Grigson, during July/August 1935. He left without paying his bill.
'a wild, unlettered and un-frenchlettered country'.
[*CL*, 190: to Bert Trick (Summer 1935)].

*County Kerry*
Visited by Dylan and Caitlin during August 1946, when on holiday with Bill and Helen McAlpine.

## EQUATOR
On the map of love the two-backed island lay on the equator.
['The Map of Love', *CS*, 109].

## EUROPE
*Letter:*
'Oh Europe etcetera please do be bettera', writes warbling Thomas during the first year of World War Two.
[*CL*, 460 (prob. 8 August 1940)].
*Works:*
(i) Under Europe is a drowned and forgotten city.
['A Prospect of the Sea', *CS*. 91].
(ii) Part of the young reporter's address.
['Old Garbo', *Portrait*, *CS*, 210].
(iii) After his fight with Dan Jenkyn, Thomas's black eye is possibly the best in Europe.
['The Fight', *Portrait*, *CS*, 154].
(iv) Where the boat takes lecturers after American tours.
['A Visit to America', *QEOM*, 64].

## FINLAND
The subject of one of the books Cribbe reads for his publishers.
['How to be a Poet', *Prospect*, 108].

## FLANDERS
'The Front . . . to which only young men travelled'.
['Reminiscences of Childhood (Second Version)', *QEOM*, 9].

## FRANCE
(i) Where they don't speak 'like that'.

['if the lady from the casino', *Notebooks*, 123].

(ii) (a) A country much liked by Mr Bennet.
(b) Where Dr Rock always wore a yachting cap.
[*The Doctor and the Devils*, Section 56, pp. 54, 55].

(iii) Where live lovers of music-making.
['The International Eisteddfod', *QEOM*, 60].

*Boulogne*
Sir Henry Price-Parry's only experience of foreign parts.
[*Rebecca's Daughters*, 10].

*Brittany*
Hearing the region's music reminds Thomas, who had never been there, of holidays in Brittany.
['The International Eisteddfod', *QEOM*, 60].

*Nice*
(i) 'An old chatterbox, barenaveled at Nice', conveys her message by stepping on the gas.
['Praise to the architects', *PDJ*, 58; *Notebooks*, 210].

(ii) Where Brazell, who mispronounced it, said he would not be holidaying.
['Extraordinary Little Cough', *Portrait*, *CS*, 169].

*Paris*
(i) Where ladies have 'a way with men'.
['The caterpillar is with child', *Notebooks*, 132].

(ii) Where the roof flacillates.
['if the lady from the casino', *Notebooks*, 122].

(iii) Thomas urges his aunt not to buy a Paris hat.
['A Letter to my Aunt', *PDJ*, 83].

(iv) The setting of a film that Salnady has enjoyed.
['Spajma and Salnady', *EP*, 142].

(v) A city Elizabeth would love to see and Dr Rock to talk about.
[*The Doctor and the Devils*, Section 56, pp. 54, 55].

(vi) Where the Surrealist Movement began.
['Poetic Manifesto', *EP*, 159].

(vii) Where Mr Weazley had been.
['A Story', *CS*, 339].

*Eiffel Tower*
Lou's room seems up as many stairs as . . .
['One Warm Saturday', *Portrait*, *CS*, 232].

*Riviera*
Mr Farr, faced with the 'Fishguard's' empty bar, wonders whether the regulars may have gone there.
['Old Garbo', *Portrait*, *CS*, 214].

*Toulouse*
Where, the poet urges, his reader should 'Tune in to a tin organ'.
['The first ten years in school and park', *Notebooks*, 194].

*Tournas, Burgundy*
Burgundians from Tournas offer a dance-version of the grape-harvest.
['The International Eisteddfod', *QEOM*, 61].

# GERMANY
See *WEST GERMANY*, below.

# GIBRALTAR
To which the City is compared.

[*The Doctor and the Devils*, Section 53, p. 50].

## GREECE
Thomas never went there and never wanted to: 'A bucket of Greek sun would drown in one colour the crowds of colours I like trying to mix for myself out of a grey flat insular mud'.
[*CL*, 266: to Lawrence Durrell (prob. December 1937)].

### Aegean
The poem is about Sophocles' *Electra*, the heroine of which has a broken heart that cannot be cooled by an Aegean wind.
['Greek Play in a Garden', *PDJ*, 57; *Notebooks*, 208].

### Salonika
Where Cyril's father went in World War One.
['The Fight', *Portrait*, *CS*, 155].

## HOLLAND
Thomas is impressed by Dutch country dances.
['The International Eisteddfod', *QEOM*, 60, 61].

## INDIA
Thomas's elder sister, Nancy, was drafted to India in 1943. There she remained with her second husband, Colonel Summersby, until her death on 16 April 1953, aged 47.
(i) To which ships sailed from Swansea Docks.
  ['Reminiscences of Childhood (Second Version)', *QEOM*, 8].
(ii) Where Anthony Raine used to live.
  [*Rebecca's Daughters*, 10, 42].
(iii) Where Hetty's uncle, Martha-the-

woolshop's husband, had been.
['The Followers', *CS*, 335].

## IRAN
The Anglo-Iranian Oil Company commissioned Thomas to script a film about oilmen to be made by a film company called Green Park. He flew to Iran on 8 January 1951 and stayed until the following month.

### Abadan
Where Thomas stayed for most of his visit.
'puking Abadan on . . . the foul blue boiling Persian buggering Gulf'.
[*CL*, 785: to an American Friend (c. January 1951)].

## IRELAND
See *EIRE*, above, and *NORTHERN IRELAND*, below.

## IRISH SEA
In which a Grecian voice spoke.
['Today, this insect', *PDJ*, 125].

## ISRAEL
Basic questions cannot be answered until Israel's voice is still.
['Why is the blood red and the grass green', *Notebooks*, 138].

### Bethlehem
(i) 'The Bethlehem under the skin' is where a baby first speaks.
  ['[Our] sun burns the morning', *Notebooks*, 238].
(ii) The gardener tells the child about Bethlehem.
  (b) The idiot repeats the name.
  (c) At Christmas, Bethlehem is

nearer than expected.
['The Tree', *CS*, 6, 9, 10].

*Calvary*
(i) The poet's youth was 'when there was grass on Calvary'.
['Into be home from home', *Notebooks*, 121].
(ii) Of which the gardener thinks.
['The Tree', *CS*, 8].

*Galilee*
Where doves are concealed.
['On the Marriage of a Virgin', *PDJ*, 170].

*Gethsemane*
The man in the pit has known the same agony.
['Out of the pit', *PDJ*, 52; *Notebooks*, 189].

*Jerusalem*
(i) Its voice cries out as the grass is slashed.
['The Holy Six', *CS*, 101].
(ii) The gardener talks of its wonders.
['The Tree', *CS*, 6].

*Judea*
Where the river does not flow on the Sabbath.
['The Crumbs of One Man's Year', *CS*, 312].


## ITALY

The Thomases lived in Italy during 1947, the visit being financed by friends and by a Society of Authors Travelling Scholarship. Elba apart, they didn't like much of it.

A country of music-lovers and music-makers.

['The International Eisteddfod', *QEOM*, 60].

*Bologna*
From which city come singers of Palestrina.
['The International Eisteddfod', *QEOM*, 60].

*Elba*
Their favourite Italian place, despite the heat. The Thomas family lived at Albergo Elba, Rio Marina, Isola d'Elba, from 20/21 July 1947 until 11 August 1947. After Dylan's death Caitlin returned to Elba to live.
(i) 'The heat! Old Elbanites on their flayed and blistered backs whimper . . . I . . . am peeling too like a drenched billboard . . . Cold beer is bottled God . . . impossible air, blister-biting blimp-blue bakehouse sea'.
[*CL*, 656-57: to Margaret Taylor (3 August 1947)].
(ii) An island 'which we love'.
[*CL*, 742: to Princess Caetani (12 January 1950)].

*Florence*
Thomas and family lived close to Florence for most of their stay in Italy (see *Mosciano*, below).

'I go, bumpy with mosquito bites, to Florence itself, which is a gruelling museum'.
[*CL*, 649: to T. W. Earp (11 July 1947)].
> *Café Giubbe Rossa, Piazza della Repubblica*
> For long a haunt of artists and writers this was Thomas's favourite place in the centre of the city.

*Elba, Italy*

*Genoa*
Thomas was fascinated by its heat, colour, dirt, noise, and washing-lines. [*CL*, 628: to Mr & Mrs D. J. Thomas (5 May 1947)].

*Italian Riviera*
'Too tidy'. [*CL*, 631: to Bill & Helen McAlpine (20 May 1947)].

*Milan*
'a giant, nightmare city'. [*CL*, 621: to Mr & Mrs D. J. Thomas (11 April 1947)].

*Mosciano*
The village five miles from and over-looking Florence in which the Thomases lived from 12 May 1947 to

20 July 1947.
*Villa del Beccaro, Mosciano, Scandicci, Florence*
The Thomas's home.

(i) 'The pooled ponded rosed goldfished arboured lizarded swinghung towelled winetabled Aeronshrill garden leads into our own (dear God) olives and vines climbing to a mutes' conventicle, a Niobe's eisteddfod, of cypresses'. [*CL*, 630: to Margaret Taylor (20 May 1947)].

(ii) 'almost a palazzo Where the people talk potato

199

And the weather drives
　　　　me pazzo'.
The Thomas family could
be found 'drinking chianti
in our marble shanty'.
[*CL*, 649: verse-letter to T.
W. Earp (11 July 1947)].

*Naples*
Artists make the sea at New Quay
seem bluer — though shallower —
than the bay of Naples.
['Quite Early One Morning', *CS*,
293].

*Pisa*
The fair-girl is 'lame like Pisa'.
['The Orchards', *CS*, 48].

*Pompeii*
'Mrs Prothero was announcing ruin
like a town crier in Pompeii'.
['A Child's Christmas in Wales', *CS*,
296].

*Rapallo*
On arriving in Italy — and before
settling in Mosciano — the Thomases
stayed in a small village one mile
from Rapallo. The latter was a smart
resort.
'women from Phillips Oppenheim,
international millionaires, & . . . us'.
[*CL*, 625: to Margaret Taylor (12
April 1947)].

*Rome*
*Letter:*
'I loved it in Rome'.
[*CL*, 649: to T. W. Earp (11 July
1947)].
*Works:*
(i)　The setting of Thomas's spoof
play, 'Lunch at Mussolini's'.
['The Sincerest Form of Flat-

tery', *EP*, 93].
(ii)　One of the places that seem like
'cobbles' in the rural tide.
['Ballad of the Long-Legged
Bait', *PDJ*, 168].

*St Peter's*
'corridors like the terraces of
Gods'.
[*CL*, 627: to Mr & Mrs D. J.
Thomas (5 May 1947)].
*Sistine Chapel*
'craning and panting in the Sis-
tine Chapel . . . wonderful'.
[*CL*, 627: to Mr & Mrs D. J.
Thomas (5 May 1947)].
*Vatican City*
'dizzily moving down marble
miles'.
[*CL*, 627: to Mr & Mrs D. J.
Thomas (5 May 1947)].

*San Michele di Pagona, Rapallo*
From early April 1947 to 12 May 1947
the Thomases lived at Villa Cuba,
their first Italian home.
'a lovely village'.
[*CL*, 622: to Mr & Mrs D. J. Thomas
(11 April 1947)].

*Sicily*
Where, said the Fat Man, there had
been a heat-wave.
['After the Fair', *CS*, 3].

*Vesuvius*
Lord Cut-Glass has 'Vesuvius clocks
all black bells and lava'.
[*UMW*, 65].

# JAMAICA
'I would take her
From here to Jamaica'
sings Augustus about Georgina Grig.

200

*[Me and My Bike, 48].*

## JAPAN
(i)   Where there had been an earthquake.
      ['The Followers', *CS*, 329].
(ii)  '. . . silky, tingling, uneasy Eastern music undoes him in a Japanese minute', First Voice reports of Nogood Boyo.
      [*UMW*, 73].

## JAVA
Where live lovers of music-making.
['The International Eisteddfod', *QEOM*, 60].

## JORDAN
(i)    The 'cavern' is the poet's 'Jordan'.
       ['The cavern shelters me from harm', *Notebooks*, 72].
(ii)   Into which the afflicted man is pushed and absorbed.
       ['Out of the pit', *PDJ*, 52, 53; *Notebooks*, 189, 191].
(iii)  The poet, before birth, was as shapeless as Jordan's water.
       ['Before I knocked', *PDJ*, 68; *Notebooks*, 231].
(iv)   The 'crossing Jordan', says the poet, waters his grave.
       ['My world is Pyramid', *PDJ*, 105].

*Dead Sea*
'the diver's bell . . .
Rings out the Dead Sea scale'.
['I, in my intricate image', *PDJ*, 110].

*Gomorrah*
(i)   To which the doctor's City is compared.
      [*The Doctor and the Devils*, Section 16, p.23].
(ii)  'Off to Gomorrah!' cries Jack

Black eagerly.
[*UMW*, 79].

*Jericho*
(i)   The destroyer of Eden.
      ['Today, this insect', *PDJ*, 124].
(ii)  Jericho fell in the lungs of whales.
      ['Ballad of the Long-Legged Bait', *PDJ*, 163].

*Shiloh*
The seed of which will not be sown in a womb.
['Shiloh's seed shall not be sewn', *Notebooks*, 229].

*Sodom*
(i)   One of the places that seem like 'cobbles' in the rural tide.
      ['Ballad of the Long-Legged Bait', *PDJ*, 168].
(ii)  To which the doctor's City is compared.
      [*The Doctor and the Devils*, Section 16, p. 23].

## KARA SEA
See *ARCTIC*, above.

## LAPLAND
(i)   Remembered Christmasses are always as snowy as Lapland.
      ['A Child's Christmas in Wales', *CS*, 296].
(ii)  To the Narrator Swansea's bombed and snowy High Street is like Lapland.
      ['Return Journey', *CS*, 316].

## MADAGASCAR
Where George Hooping's father saw a killer whale.

['Extraordinary Little Cough', *Portrait*, *CS*, 166].

## MAJORCA
Where, according to Thomas, Sidney Salt conducted his intellectual life. Thomas reviewed a volume of Salt's verse in the *Adelphi*.
['To Pamela Hansford Johnson', *EP*, 139].

## MEDITERRANEAN
(i)  One of the Fat Man's topics of conversation.
['After the Fair', *CS*, 3].
(ii)  Retired sea-captains drown in cabins of sleep that are as blue as the Mediterranean.
['Quite Early One Morning', *CS*, 291].

## NORTHERN IRELAND
*Bangor, County Down*
Listed under 'B' in the schoolchildren's alphabet-song about places with race-tracks.
[*Me and My Bike*, 39].

*Belfast*
Where young Thomas would have a fight.
['Who Do You Wish Was With Us?', *Portrait*, *CS*, 201].

## NORWAY
Where live lovers of music-making.
['The International Eisteddfod', *QEOM*, 60].

## PERSIA
See *IRAN*, above.

## POLAND
Where Hugo de Hugo's mother came from.
['The Sincerest Form of Flattery', *EP*, 91].

## RUSSIA
The setting of Thomas's short novel-parody.
['The Sincerest Form of Flattery', *EP*, 90].

*Moscow*
Which Ted Jenkins fails to find on his radio set.
['The Londoner', *The Doctor and the Devils and Other Scripts*, 219].

*Russian Seas*
Whose legends died as the trees blazed.
['The Orchards', *CS*, 42].

*Sea of Azov*
Beside which a woman wailed.
['The Orchards', *CS,* 42].

*Siberia*
In Swansea's bombed and wintry High Street the snowflakes are like 'Siberian confetti'.
['Return Journey', *CS*, 316].

## SAHARA
See *AFRICA*, above.

## SARGASSO SEA
(i)  'The dry Sargasso of the tomb'.
['When once the twilight locks no longer', *PDJ*, 97; *Notebooks*, 256 — mis-spelled as 'Sargossa'].
(ii)  The sea that watered the bare feet of time's effigy.
['The Mouse and the Woman', *CS*, 84].

## SCOTLAND

*Balmoral Castle*
A conventional painting of the castle is, for Thomas, a symbol of artistic worthlessness.
['To Pamela Hansford Johnson', *EP*, 131].

*Edinburgh*
Thomas took part in 'Tributes to Hugh Macdiarmid' at the 1948 Edinburgh Festival.
Where one of Thomas's class-mates had been.
['The Fight', *Portrait*, *CS*, 155].

*Perth*
Where the Dougals lived, whose son married Phoebe Mary Quincey.
['The End of the River', *CS*, 50].

## SHETLAND ISLANDS
(i)  Shetland ponies scampered on fairgrounds.
['Holiday Memory', *CS*, 309].
(ii)  Upper-class English lecturers sometimes talk to women's clubs in America on aspects of the islands.
['A Visit to America', *QEOM*, 64].

## SOUTH AMERICA
Which Ted Jackson fails to find on his radio set.
['The Londoner', *The Doctor and the Devils and Other Scripts*, 219].

## SOUTH SEA
(i)  The dying Peter imagines a beautiful tropical island.
['The Visitor', *CS*, 26].
(ii)  The 'basin of the South' helps water the poet's grave.

['My World is Pyramid', *PDJ*, 105].
(iii)  The setting of *The Beach of Falesá*.

## SPAIN
Where live lovers of music-making.
['The International Eisteddfod', *QEOM*, 60].

## SWITZERLAND
Where live lovers of music-making.
['The International Eisteddfod', *QEOM*, 60].

*Alps*
(i)  Welsh children play on 'raven Alps' (i.e. coal-tips).
['The first ten years in school and park', *Notebooks*, 193].
(ii)  Which whales resemble.
['Ballad of the Long-Legged Bait', *PDJ*, 163].

*Matterhorn*
One of Salnady's ambitions is to see a 'crippled yoddler throwing almanacks from the top of the Matterhorn'.
['Spajma and Salnady', *EP*, 145].

## TAHITI
(i)  Rhianon has Tahitian-like warming qualities.
['The Visitor', *CS*, 25].
(ii)  The woman is charmed by 'Enamoured Tahiti'.
['Into her lying down head', *LVW*, 93; not in *PDJ* version)].

## TRINIDAD
The subject of water-colours found in Welsh bedrooms.
['Quite Early One Morning', *CS*, 292].

## WEST GERMANY

'Germany' is the only foreign station that
Ted Jackson can receive on his radio set.
['The Londoner', *The Doctor and the Devils
and Other Scripts*, 219].

> *Bonn*
> Where Cedric went for his holidays,
> after considering the Rhondda.
> ['How to be a Poet', *Prospect*, 112].

> *Obernkirchen*
> Whose children's choir sing like 'pig-
> tailed angels'.
> ['The International Eisteddfod',
> *QEOM*, 61].

## ZANZIBAR

The name of Nogood Boyo's dinghy.
[*UMW*, 2, 37, 72].

# PHOTOGRAPHS & MAPS

The author and publishers wish to thank the following people and institutions for their photographs:

Amherst College Library 178; BBC Hulton Library 138, 139, 147, 149; Boston University 181; Chicago University 182; Messrs. Cornish and Birtill 161; Fotowales 50, 71, 97, 98, 99, 100, 117, 118, 121, 122, 124, 129; John Ganz 24, 27, 33, 37, 40, 41, 47, 51, 52, 55, 57, 59, 62, 68; Iowa State University 184; Italian Institute 199; Keith Johnson 126; Major J. T. Kelly 159; Magdalen College, Oxford 160; New York Public Library 166, 167, 170, 171, 173; San Francisco State University 186; N. W. Seymour 169, 172; Swansea City Council 18 (Map), 25, 26, 28, 29, 30, 31, 34, 35, 42, 44, 45, 46, 49, 53, 54, 56, 58, 61, 63, 64, 65, 66, 67, 69, 70, 72, 73, 74, 75, 88; Lee Tucker 86, 87, 137, 140, 142, 144, 146; University of California, Berkeley 181; University of Washington 187; Roger Vlitos 38, 90, 94, 95, 96, 97, 98, 99, 100, 101, 111; Welsh Office 113; Westminster City Library 143, 145, 150; and HMSO, Ordnance Survey and Geographers A–Z on which the maps on pages 76, 77, 78, 79, 80, 81 and 132 were based.

# EXPLANATORY NOTES

The following material is listed:

1. All places of biographical importance.
2. The most important topographical references in Dylan Thomas's published letters, using *The Collected Letters,* ed. Paul Ferris (Dent, 1985). If no correspondent is named the letter is to Vernon Watkins.
3. All topographical references in the following volumes or parts of volumes, using the cited editions:

   (a) *The Doctor and the Devils* (Dent, 1953).
   (b) 'A Dream of Winter' and 'The Londoner', *The Doctor and the Devils and Other Scripts* (New York: New Directions, 1953; repr. as ND Paperbook, 1970), pp. 207-8, 213-29.
   (c) *Under Milk Wood* (Dent, 1954; repr. 1957).
   (d) *Quite Early One Morning* (Dent, 1954; repr. as Aldine Paperback, 1971).

   Material from this volume is listed only when it does not appear in (j) or (l) below. Further:

   (i) Except for the opening description of Swansea 'Reminiscences of Swansea (First Version)' has been ignored in favour of the second version.
   (ii) 'Memories of Christmas' became part of 'A Child's Christmas in Wales' (included in (l), below). I have used material from the former only when it does not also appear in the latter.
   (iii) Of the pieces in Part II of Dent's edition of *Quite Early One Morning* I have included material from only two: 'The English Festival of Spoken Poetry' and 'Wales and the Artist'. Topographical material in the other pieces invariably relates to the lives and works of other writers.

   (e) *Quite Early One Morning* (New York: New Directions, 1954).

   This edition is substantially different from Dent's. I have only included material from pp. 89-93 — Thomas's film-script, 'Our Country' — which is not found elsewhere.

   (f) *A Prospect of the Sea,* ed. Daniel Jones (Dent, 1955; repr. 1960).

   Material from this volume is included only when it does not also appear in (l), below. Further:

   (i) 'Conversations about Christmas' became part of 'A Child's Christmas in Wales' (included in (l), below). I have included material from the former only when it does not also appear in the latter.

(g) *Me and My Bike* (Triton, 1965).

(h) *Rebecca's Daughters* (Triton, 1965).

(i) *Poet in the Making: The Notebooks of Dylan Thomas*, ed. Ralph Maud (Dent, 1968).

(j) *The Poems*, ed. Daniel Jones (Dent, 1971; repr. as Everyman Paperback, 1982). All editions of *The Poems* have the same pagination but editions from 1978 onwards include an additional poem — 'A Pub Poem' — in an appendix.

(k) *Early Prose Writings*, ed. Walford Davies (Dent, 1971).

Material from this volume is included only when it does not appear in (l), below. Further, I have *not* included material from the following pieces:

pp. 67-73    excerpts from *The Death of the King's Canary*. Thomas wrote this jointly with John Davenport and their respective contributions cannot be distinguished.

(For the same reason I have not included material from the complete novel published by Hutchinson in 1976.)

pp. 97-121    'The Poets of Swansea'.

pp. 122-24    'Genius and Madness Akin in World of Art'.

pp. 165-204    'Reviews'.

(l) *The Collected Stories* (Dent, 1983).

This edition collects all Thomas's published fiction.

4.  The following references from Thomas's adaptations of short stories by, respectively, Robert Louis Stevenson and Maurice O'Sullivan.

(a) *The Beach of Falesá* (Cape, 1964): the setting (Chapter Nine / SOUTH SEA) and two references that seem Thomas's own (see Chapter One / *Old Red Cow* and Chapter Four / *Works*, xvi).

(b) *Twenty Years A'Growing* (Dent, 1964): the settings (Chapter Nine / EIRE / *Blasket Islands* and EIRE / *Dingle, County Kerry*).

*Additional Information*

Page numbers refer to the above editions but the aim throughout this book is to provide sufficient information to enable readers with other editions to track down references as easily as possible.

In each entry references are listed in chronological order of composition (if known) or publication.

Wherever possible the spelling of Welsh place-names follows Thomas's own usage.

# ABBREVIATIONS

| | |
|---|---|
| CL | *The Collected Letters,* ed. Paul Ferris. |
| CS | *The Collected Stories.* |
| EP | *Early Prose Writings*, ed. Walford Davies. |
| LVW | *Letters to Vernon Watkins.* |
| Notebooks | *Poet in the Making: The Notebooks of Dylan Thomas*, ed. Maud. |
| PDJ | *The Poems*, ed. Daniel Jones. |
| Portrait | *Portrait of the Artist as a Young Dog,* included in *The Collected Stories.* |
| Prospect | *A Prospect of the Sea.* |
| QEOM | *Quite Early One Morning* (Dent). |
| QEOM (USA) | *Quite Early One Morning* (New York: New Directions). |
| ST | *Adventures in the Skin Trade,* included in *The Collected Stories.* |
| UMW | *Under Milk Wood.* |

# FURTHER READING

ACKERMAN, John,
*Dylan Thomas: His Life and Work* (O.U.P., 1964).
*Welsh Dylan,* (Cardiff: John Jones, 1979; repr. as Paladin Paperback, Granada, 1980).

BRINNIN, John Malcolm,
*Dylan Thomas in America* (Dent, 1956).

DAVIES, Walford,
*Dylan Thomas,* 'Writers of Wales' Series (Cardiff: Un. of Wales Press, 1972).

FERRIS, Paul,
*Dylan Thomas* (Hodder & Stoughton, 1977; repr. as Penguin Paperback, 1978).

FITZGIBBON, Constantine,
*The Life of Dylan Thomas* (Dent, 1965).

GINGERICH, Martin E.,
'Dylan Thomas and America', *Dylan Thomas Remembered* (Swansea: The Dylan Thomas Society Wales Branch, 1978), pp. 26-34.

JONES, Daniel,
*My Friend Dylan Thomas* (Dent, 1977).

LEWIS, Min,
*Laugharne and Dylan Thomas* (Dobson, 1967).

READ, Bill,
*The Days of Dylan Thomas* (Weidenfeld & Nicholason, 1964).

SEYMOUR, Tryntje Van Ness,
*Dylan Thomas' New York* (Owings Mills, Maryland: Stemmer House, 1978).

SINCLAIR, Andrew,
*Dylan Thomas: Poet of His People* (Michael Joseph, 1975).

STEAD, Peter,
'The Swansea of Dylan Thomas', *Dylan Thomas Remembered* (Swansea: The Dylan Thomas Society Wales Branch, 1978), pp. 8-25.

TEDLOCK, E. W. (editor),
*Dylan Thomas: The Legend and the Poet* (Heinemann, 1960).

THOMAS, Caitlin,
*Leftover Life to Kill* (Putnam, 1957).

WATKINS, Gwen,
*Portrait of a Friend* (Llandysul: Gomer Press, 1983).